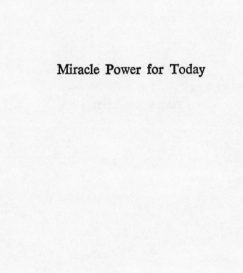

Miracle Power for Today

By the Same Author

FOCUS ON LIVING

Miracle Power for Today

WINIFRED WILKINSON

DOUBLEDAY & COMPANY, INC., GARDEN CITY, NEW YORK   1969

Library of Congress Catalog Card Number 76–79968
Copyright © 1969 by Winifred Wilkinson
All Rights Reserved
Printed in the United States of America
First Edition

To
my husband
GEORGE HAUSMANN
who shares
so many miracles
with me

Contents

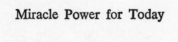

Miracle Power for Today

Introduction

Miracles happen every day, somewhere, to someone. They can happen to you!

Wonders not only can happen, but they do happen to those who are willing to believe in them and to work intelligently with the power which brings them about.

This book is designed to acquaint you with this miracle power and to share with you some of the methods which you can use to make your own miracles.

Do you know what a miracle is? Would you recognize one if you saw it?

Webster defines a miracle as "an event or action that apparently contradicts known scientific laws" (Webster's New World Dictionary, Concise Edition, 1958, p. 478). The key word is "apparently."

Nothing can contradict the basic laws under which the universe operates, but not all of these laws are as yet understood by man. Many of them are just beginning to be probed and studied by the scientists. Still others must await man's greater ability to understand.

But the laws continue to operate, whether or not man comprehends them. They work for him, or against him, according to the way he activates them in his life.

The laws are at work in your life. They are activated in many ways, by your thoughts, your feelings, your attitudes, your reactions to life, and so on. They can be activated by your own conscious acceptance and use of the miracle power God has given you. When they are, the unusual will become usual for you, the exceptions will single you out of the crowd, and miracles will happen, not once in a while, but frequently in your life.

The principle of the miracle is this:

The universe is governed by law. Those laws which are now understood are subject to higher laws and other principles. When it appears that a known law has been broken, it simply means that another, higher law has been invoked, one which nullifies the results which would normally be expected.

Man could have learned to fly thousands of years ago, but he believed himself held fast to the earth. Discovery of the law of gravity pretty well convinced him that he was supposed to be earth-bound. But always there were those who continued to believe in miracles and who searched for the working of a higher law which would nullify the law of gravity.

Someone discovered the principle of aerodynamics, one of those little-understood higher laws, and man learned that, by working with this law, he could fly!

Whenever he sees a higher principle at work, man cries, "Miracle!" because he doesn't understand it.

There are other laws that are just beginning to be explored. There are laws of mind, principles of growth, spiritual truths and other higher, more powerful governing laws.

This book will introduce you to some of these miracle-working ideas which will help you to be happier, healthier and more prosperous. It will give you foundation principles for meeting situations that arise in life and changing them. It will introduce you to miracle power, which can lead you into a discovery and understanding of new and greater laws.

This is your invitation to make your own miracles. Learn these universal principles, work with them, open the way for miracle power to change your life, and wonders will happen to you!

Chapter 1

Plug in the Miracle Power

You not only have a powerhouse working for you night and day, but you are a powerhouse. Plug in to the Source; acknowledge, accept and use your own miracle power, and you will have all the riches of mind, body and affairs you can ever use.

You are a physical powerhouse, a dynamo of vitality and energy. Your body has within it atomic power which, if it could be released, would equal the power of ten bombs the size of the one which destroyed Hiroshima.

You are a mental powerhouse—a colossus of understanding, vital information, and untapped resources beyond measure. Your mind is alive with miracle power, waiting to be released in creative activity beyond anything you have even dreamed possible.

You are a powerhouse of talent and ability, "go-power" unlimited. You not only can dream and hope and think. You can accomplish things that you may have been sure were impossible—at least for you.

You are a spiritual powerhouse, alive with the power to heal and be healed, to prosper, to succeed, and, above all, to live joyously and productively all your life.

Once you recognize this powerhouse within you and plug in the miracle power, you will go!

Learn to direct and use the power wisely, and you will find

that health, joy and accomplishment beyond your wildest imagining become the order of the day.

Plug in the power, and prepare for miracles!

An Engineering Miracle

One of the greatest engineering miracles in the world, certainly one that is beyond man's present ability to understand or even describe, is the marvel of your body, the physical mechanism through which you do many things every day and which, usually, you simply take for granted.

Consider the many things your body does even without your instruction or supervision. An intricately balanced timing system keeps your heart pumping blood throughout your body, performing all sorts of functions which you don't understand at all. It builds, cleanses, nourishes, and it does it all silently and in perfect order, except when you in some way interfere with the built-in computer that is in charge.

The body breathes for you, digests for you, and does all manner of intricate, complicated jobs for you, while you go about your business, most of the time forgetting completely that you even have a body.

But you do have a body, and if you would continue to have it perform miracles for you, you must learn to care for it and plug in your physical powerhouse to the Source of energy and vitality, intelligence and direction, for the best continuing results.

One key to greater physical health and well-being is found in the application of the law of recognition and appreciation. You open the channels for more power to flow when you begin by recognizing the miracle that your body represents, the miracle that it is by its very being.

Could you build a human body? Could you duplicate even one tiny phase of its complicated operation? Can you even see an atom, the infinitesimal source of power which is duplicated octillions of times in your body mechanism?

Wonderful things happen in your mind when you begin to see, and appreciate, this vehicle through which you express yourself every day. And those things which take place in your mind determine what your body will be to you. It can be an asset, or it can be a burden. It can be a joy, or it can be a misery to you—depending on the way you think about it, and the extent to which you are willing to accept the blessing of the miracles it provides.

Recognize the potential of your body for perfect expression and identify with the idea of the built-in intelligence that operates your body perfectly, and you will have greater health than you ever imagined possible. But disparage your body, complain about its functions, and detail its difficulties, and even the miracle of divine operation can't get through to provide strength or health.

Your body will serve you according to the way in which you program its computer with your thoughts and feelings.

Expect from it health and strength, vitality and verve, and you will see all of the fibers of your being respond to your thought and jump to fulfill your will of health.

Think health. Identify with health. Feel health. Recognize the potential of health in your built-in powerhouse of a physical body, and you will find yourself instantly strengthened. Continue to recognize your body's built-in power to express health, and you will see your whole being plugged in to the universal Source, so that you are filled with all that you need to express life, health and general well-being.

A miracle? It is something that can't be completely explained based on man's present understanding of the marvel of the human body, but it works!

This is the principle of recognition:

Recognition of the miracle power available to you is the switch that activates your powerhouse and makes you an outlet for all the power you can use at any given time.

Think of yourself as you are, a veritable powerhouse, breathing in quadrillions of oxygen atoms to replenish the supply needed by your body, breathing out quadrillions of molecules of carbon dioxide to free you from the waste.

Remember the ability of your own atomic-power plant to renew itself continually. Scientists estimate that the entire body is replaced by new material, new bones, new muscles, new atoms throughout, every five years. Most of the body is renewed within a two-year interval.

Consider the fact that the tiniest complete electric-power plant in existence is the living cell—and your body is made up of trillions of them. One laboratory connected with space exploration is now looking for ways of releasing the energy in living cells as usable electric power. But you can release power and energy in your body simply by recognizing it, believing in it, and thus calling it forth to work for you as living power.

You are the powerhouse!

Every time you disparage your body, you shut off the power, but when you recognize the power potential and literally call it forth through the activity of your mind, you have plugged into something tremendous.

Plug in the miracle power for yourself. Flip the switch in your mind, and you turn on a dynamo in your body.

Do it by claiming something like this: "I recognize that my body is a powerhouse, filled with vitality and energy at all times. I plug in this miracle power now."

Then do what you say. Literally call forth the greater supply of strength and health that is now generated in and through the powerhouse of your body. Believe in it, think about it, accept it, and be the physical powerhouse you are designed to be.

Miracle-Powered Healing

Even when there is a deep-seated need for healing, the law works, and the miracle-powered mechanism of your body responds to your recognition that it is there.

If you have become absorbed in a particular illness or physical difficulty, it means that you have forgotten that your body has a built-in repair system, one that defies man's imagination to describe. But it is there, and it works—when you remember it, recognize its latent power, and plug it in to the Source.

"The things which are impossible with men are possible with God." (Luke 18:27 ASV) And the things which seem impossible to the human mind become possible when higher laws are activated, even through an impetus as simple as the recognition of the built-in intelligence in every cell, the power to heal itself according to its own individual pattern.

Say for yourself, "I recognize and call forth the built-in Intelligence which has power to heal my body now. I plug in the power and expect miracles."

Concentrate on this idea until you really believe, you identify with it, you know it, and the healing work will be done, finished, accomplished.

I can't tell you exactly how it works, and even though you have the experience of awakening the healing power to small or large miracles in your life, you may not be able to explain it. But it is enough to know that it does work!

Many physicians state openly today that while they must give a certain prognosis in specified diseases, based on their scientific knowledge, they are well aware that the patient can activate other practically unknown healing forces by his own attitude.

In other words, ask for a miracle through your recognition of the body's own repair system, and you can have it.

Add a Dose of Appreciation

If you would rouse your body to even greater effort in the job of renewing, repairing, strengthening and vitalizing itself, go even further. Don't stop with recognition of your built-in powerhouse, with all of its intelligence and ability to do, but go one step beyond. Add a big dose of appreciation to the cure.

Chances are you have taken your body for granted most of your life. Undoubtedly there have been times when you have abused it, carried it beyond the extremes of fatigue and frustration, and generally continued to call on it without any consideration for its needs or requirements.

Many times you have forgotten about your physical powerhouse except when it, for some reason, failed to serve you as you had expected. Then your thoughts were derogatory and perhaps even more demanding of the utmost of physical effort. They were thoughts that recognized, not the potential, but the problem.

If you are going to be healed, you must stop concentrating on the problem and go back to the Source, stop emphasizing the difficulty and start appreciating that which you are and the wonderful equipment which you have to work for you.

Plug in to your miracle power with the connection of appreciation, and see it appreciate for you.

The word "appreciate" means "to recognize gratefully" (Webster's New World Dictionary, Concise Edition, p. 35), but it also means "to rise in value" (Webster's New World Dictionary, Concise Edition, p. 36). These two meanings indicate the way in which the law of appreciation works to provide miracles in your life.

The principle of appreciation is this:

That which is appreciated appreciates in value.

Stop looking to anything that is not quite right in your body, and start appreciating, in the sense of recognizing gratefully, the many wonderful ways in which this physical powerhouse serves you, and you will see it appreciate, in the sense of increasing the value, the good, the power that it is already expressing. This is a law that makes miracles everyday happenings in your life.

It works, when you work with it!

If you are concerned about some organ which is not functioning properly, or if you have been told that some disease is active in your body, take your attention away from the thing that appears to be wrong and appreciate the many things that are right.

Recognize, with the increased power of gratitude, the many miracles which your body is already, even now, providing for you, regardless of whatever seems to be wrong. When you stop to look and appreciate, you'll be surprised at the number of small miracles that you have taken for granted and ignored entirely. Stop now, and appreciate them.

Maybe you can't see perfectly. Stop fighting the difficulty—this only robs you of power. But consider the wonderful gift of hearing, or taste, or touch or any of the other services which your body is rendering perfectly. Any one provides a miracle in itself.

Appreciate the miracle. Appreciate the power that is pouring through a particular function of your body. Appreciate the flow of current that you have, and you open the switch for more miracle power to come in.

And while you are appreciating your hearing, or any of the other services your body performs perfectly, you may be surprised to find that your sight has improved, too. That is the power of appreciation, just one of the many miracles that happen when you work with the higher laws of the universe.

Direct-Current Healing

Now open the way for even more direct current to heal the problem, whatever it is. Appreciate the built-in intelligence of even those cells and atoms which are the seat of your physical difficulty. Appreciate the good that is there, concentrate on it instead of the difficulty, and watch the dynamo pour ever-increasing power into the problem, until it is healed completely.

Say, "I appreciate the miracles happening in me now, and I see them appreciated. I am now plugging in the miracle power!"

Think of what this means to you as you concentrate on the grateful acknowledgment of that which you do have in the miracle department. You may be surprised at how quickly you get results.

Don't even hold the thought that you must wait through a certain period to see something happen. Plug in the power, turn the switch, and the dynamo goes to work, providing power to fill your needs.

This same method will work even when there is no need for healing. You can increase your supply of health, strength, vitality, energy and any other good by appreciating that which you have.

Never claim weakness or lack if you would have your powerhouse operate at full strength.

Rather, concentrate all your attention on that which you want to increase.

Claim, "I appreciate perfect health in my mind, body and affairs. I plug in to this power now." Then devote all of your attention to doing just that. Let all thoughts of physical inadequacy or weakness be dissolved by your appreciation of strength, vitality and health.

That's all you have to do. The law of appreciation does the rest.

Plug in the power of your physical body through recognizing and appreciating the good you are now expressing, and prepare for miracles!

Turn on the Mental Power

Your mental powerhouse is connected by knowing that you know, recognizing that there is a Source of knowledge within you that can supply whatever answer you seek.

The miracle power that flows through your mind is tremendous, but all too often the power is dammed up or short-circuited by the human concept of not knowing, not having the answer you seek. To say "I don't know" is like throwing a monkey wrench into the works.

Your mind responds to your command. Tell it that you don't understand or can't remember, that you don't know and don't expect to know, and it simply makes that true for you. But imbue it with the idea that you do know and remember easily, turn on all the switches of recognition, and you can relax and let the miracle power flow through you to tell you everything you need to know at this particular time. Turn on the current, and all the knowledge that you can use flows through the powerhouse of your mind.

The knowing of past years, stored in your subconscious mind, is much greater than you realize. Claiming that you do know and turning the switch on your memory brings forth mental energy and know-how that you have long since forgotten you had.

To call forth knowledge you once had, based on past experience or learning, put your mind to work for you by declaring, "I recognize that I have the power to remember perfectly. I plug in this miracle power now."

Program the computer of your mind with the idea that the information stored there comes forth easily on your demand, and then forget it for the moment. As the power begins to flow, the answer will come forth so easily that you will wonder how you ever doubted in the first place.

Never apologize for a lack of the knowledge you need. Just saying the words out loud shuts down your power plant, and no matter how clear the understanding may be in your inner mind, it can't come through to fill the void. Rather, recognize that the knowledge is there, and then quietly wait until it comes through, trusting the stored information to respond to your command of recognition.

Know the Unknown

Even those things which you have never known that you knew are available to you when the power is turned on.

Where do you think inventors get their knowledge? Why do scientists try things that have never been tried before? Where does the latest knowledge, the scientific discovery of the day, originate?

It comes through the mental powerhouse of minds that are open to understanding and knowledge above and beyond anything they have ever known before.

Miracles happen to those who believe in them. And miracles of the mind come forth for those who believe that there is a Source of knowledge which is able to reveal to them all that they need to know, that is even now seeking to give them greater understanding, greater knowledge and mental power beyond man's present imagining.

How does it work? I can't tell you exactly, but I can tell you the power that activates this flow of mental current. It is the power of recognizing the Source, knowing that there is a Spirit in you that knows new and wonderful truths beyond your intellectual knowledge of the present. It is the power that claims "I do know" over and over until the answer comes through. It is the persistence that refuses to admit defeat, but continues to plug into the power of recognition, the recognition of the mental powerhouse within that knows no limitation.

Say to yourself, and mean it, "I recognize the Source of unlimited knowing within me. I plug in the miracle power to receive all that I am ready to know now."

You can't accept all mental power at once; your mental powerhouse wouldn't be able to handle it. But you will receive it as you are ready for it, as you turn on the switch and let the knowing come, the understanding unfold.

Never say "I don't know" to anyone about anything in any way, shape or form. Regardless of what you think at the present time, if you do truly desire to, and need to know, you can open the way for the mental power to flow when you claim that the Source of all knowledge does know and reveals to you that which you are ready to know now.

Don't even say weakly "I wish I knew, but I don't." Tell yourself clearly and plainly that you are recognizing your ability to know, and you will know. Something in the power of recognition turns the switch that opens the way for all knowledge to come to you.

Appreciation Increases Knowledge

Prepare for increased mental power as you employ the law of appreciation.

Saying "I don't know" is, in a sense, depreciating even that information that you have at hand. But once you plug in the power of appreciation and recognize with gratitude the great stores of knowledge which are already yours, you are in business as a mental powerhouse.

The more you appreciate your present volume of knowledge, the more it appreciates for you.

Have you ever had ideas flowing through your mind so rapidly that you found it impossible to write them down? Have you ever been so filled with exciting new possibilities that you could hardly wait to experiment with them, to see them work?

If not, then you have not been using your mind power to its greatest potential. Your mind is prepared and equipped to provide you with all the current, all the ideas, all the understanding that you can accept and use at this present time. It will increase its output as you increase your ability to receive and use the ideas it pours out to you. It is your mental powerhouse, and you are the one who sets the limit for the mental energy produced. It can be just as much as you are prepared to receive and to use.

Appreciate the knowledge you now have, endow it with increased value as you give thanks for it, and there is no limit to what you can comprehend as you open all the switches and let your mental dynamo operate at full power.

The miracle of mind power begins when you turn on the switch of recognition and appreciation, and let the power flow!

Talents, Unlimited

Let the energy of your mind overflow into your powerhouse of talent and ability, and you will be surprised at the things that can be accomplished by you, achievements that are beyond your present ability to conceive. But they are there, waiting for you to throw the switch and let the miracle power come through in the form of talent, ability and enthusiasm to express them.

What would you like to do? What talents have you always envied in others? What have you wistfully considered a hopeless, but desirable, goal?

You don't have to spend your life on the sidelines, watching others accomplish the things that you would like to do. Plug in the power for the expression of your own latent talent and ability, and see your most cherished dreams come true.

Do it first by recognizing that you are a powerhouse of talent and ability. You have a potentiality beyond anything you have ever begun to express in your life. You can do things greater than anything you even dreamed of doing. Don't shut off the miracle power by saying "can't." Open yourself to new possibilities, new areas for exploration, new ways of doing things, and new things to do.

From By-lines to Headlines

As a professional writer, for many years I said glibly, "I'd rather have a by-line than a headline any day." And for years I had by-lines as a reward for writing talent.

But when I began to discover new areas of expression, I opened the switches and let the power come through for the development of other talents and abilities, activities I had never even considered as a part of my professional life. And I found there was nothing wrong with headlines as a recognition of my work as a public speaker and ordained minister.

Surprises are in store for the one who turns on the miracle power of divine energy to develop new areas for the expression of talents as yet undiscovered and unknown.

When I first became interested in these universal principles and their application to the life of the individual, I had a deep desire to tell others of them. Pretty soon, I discovered that it wasn't enough to be writing about them—I wanted to communicate these ideas in other ways.

And so I plugged in the miracle power and learned to do things I had never considered possible. I learned to speak in public by recognizing that there was a Power within me that could do it. I learned to employ these principles in a counseling service. I started a daily radio program, writing the script and giving the broadcast. I became an ordained minister, performing weddings, conducting funerals, doing things that I had never dreamed of doing in my wildest imaginings—and loving every minute of it.

This is what life is like when you plug in the miracle power for creative, constructive living, and the development of new and untried capabilities and capacities. And you can do it!

Your desires and trends of interest will be your own, and they are the guidelines you should follow in determining what you want to do and the way you want to go.

But you are unlimited! Recognize that you have the latent ability now to do things you have never dreamed possible, and you have taken the first step to open the channels and let the power flow.

Your desires, your interests and your deep-down yearnings are guideposts along the path of accomplishment that you are ready to travel at this particular time in your life.

Take their direction; then plug in the power by recognizing that what you can visualize, you can do. What you can see yourself accomplishing, you can accomplish. What you want to do badly enough, you will do. And all the power you can ever use will be poured out to help you do it.

Employ the law of recognition by selling yourself on this idea:

"There is a miracle power within me that can accomplish all things through me. I now plug in this power, and I am unlimited!"

Let yourself dwell on this idea until you really believe it, you see yourself doing things you have never done before, and not only that, but you feel the energy and the push that impel you forward into doing it.

This is the key to your powerhouse of talent and ability. Turn the key, and let the miracles happen through you!

Be the Best!

Even your present abilities can be increased and animated and activated beyond your greatest dreams. Those talents which you are now using and those capabilities which you are now expressing represent only a small part of your total capacity to do those particular things.

Turn the switch, let the miracle power flow in greater and greater volume, and you will be surprised at the ease and joy with which you become not only better, but the best in your chosen fields of endeavor.

Don't ever be satisfied just to do a particular job well. This is good, but not good enough for you! Strive to be the best! Learn how to work with joy and ease, and don't stop working until you reach the pinnacle. When you do, you'll begin to see new mountains to climb and new fields to conquer. Climb them! Conquer them! Keep growing and developing all your abilities all your life.

Increase your power to produce good on your present level of expression by appreciating that which you can do now at this particular time.

Some women can't even accept a compliment on a pie well baked. They begin to speak of trouble with the oven or mention that the crust wasn't just right.

Don't be completely satisfied with what you are doing. If you are, you will never try to do more. But don't disparage your present efforts either. Appreciate the power that is using your particular channels for expression at this particular time, and see it appreciate as you open the way for more to come.

Indeed, you can be better. You can do better. But you will do it much more quickly and surely by giving thanks for the abilities you are now using and letting them grow for you.

That which is appreciated, appreciates! This is a law, and it works for abilities as for anything else.

Claim something like this: "I will give thanks that I can do this thing well, and I prepare the way for greater success and accomplishment by plugging in the miracle power now!"

Then do it. Don't be satisfied to stop where you are, but do give thanks for, and appreciate, the progress you have made so far.

Miracles on the Ladder of Success

And you don't have to wait for someone to die to move up on the ladder of success and accomplishment.

Many people limit themselves by looking around and seeing only certain opportunities. Instead of concentrating on developing their particular capabilities, literally turning on the power in themselves, they look over the situation and say, "When So-and-So dies, I'll be able to move up to vice-president. For the present, I'll have to stay where I am." They dig their own rut, when they could be building a power plant, producing miracles all the time.

For you there is a right place. For you there is a right expression of talent. For you there is a right pay, a right reward for services rendered.

If you are content to stay in one place, doing nothing to increase your power of service or ability to do things well, then your place may continue to be just where you are—even when So-and-So dies.

But if you will make up your mind to appreciate your output, to increase your ability to do present jobs and others well, you will discover that there is a right place for you higher on the ladder of success—and it will pay accordingly. Refuse to limit yourself by thinking that you can only move in one direction. Appreciate your present abilities, and then leave all the doors open for your highest good.

Prepare for miracles, and expect them to happen!

Recognize! Appreciate! These two words are the keys to the opening of unlimited power lines for your good.

The Greatest Powerhouse of All

So far we have considered the way in which these two acts work to increase your output of physical power so that your body can be a dynamo of energy, strength and vitality. Use the force of recognition to know and feel the tremendous latent power in every cell and atom of your physical body. Recognize it, appreciate it, praise this potential and then let the miracle power flow to make you whole and well, dynamic and vital every moment of your life.

We talked about your mental powerhouse, that colossus of understanding that can open the way to knowledge as yet unimagined even in your wildest daydreams. Again, the key is recognition and appreciation. Recognize that there is a power in you that knows—knows everything you can ever need to know. Call on this power for recall or memory and also for new ideas, new concepts, new understanding. Do it through recognizing that it is there and appreciating that which you do know now. Don't limit yourself, but turn the current on full as you recognize and appreciate the mental power you have.

Next we took up the latent power in talents and abilities, things you have not yet tried and other abilities crying to be increased and improved in your everyday experience. Again, the key is recognition and appreciation. Recognize that you can do all things when you turn on your built-in powerhouse, and turn the switch with appreciation until the powerhouse of talent is running at full capacity.

Now we come to another powerhouse. Here, too, the key is recognition and appreciation. But this particular part of your nature is above and beyond anything even the physical, the mental or the talent powerhouse can produce. And it contributes its volume of output to all of the others. This is the powerhouse of the Spirit. Some call it universal power.

People have many words for this phase of your life. What you call it is not as important as your recognition and appreciation of it.

A Spiritual Powerhouse—Unlimited!

Many people today seem almost afraid to say the word "God." They hesitate to mention prayer or to think in terms of living by spiritual laws, thinking that they will be laughed at by their friends, or will be misfits in their world because others don't understand.

If you refuse to turn on your spiritual powerhouse simply because of what others will think, then you are missing the greatest opportunity of your life.

Don't call it spiritual power if this offends your sensibilities in some way. Do as many do. Speak of Nature if you don't want to say "God." Talk of universal principles, and universal power, or miracle power, if you don't want to use the word "spiritual."

But, whatever you call it, turn on the spiritual power in your life if you want to make miracles happen! Turn it on and let it flow, and you will be amazed at the things that can happen to you.

You will be richer—in mind, body and affairs. You will be happier in every way. You will be wiser and stronger and more competent and all of the other things you want to be. You will have miracle power working for you to establish your greatest heart's desires of good, when you learn to live in the spiritual powerhouse that you are, and to turn on even a fraction of the current that is available to you.

To a certain extent, the techniques already discussed to release the power in body, mind and activity have given you an introduction to the vital energy that is potentially yours.

Now really turn on the miracle power, and let it flow, by using the same two principles in prayer.

Recognize that there is a Presence and a Power, an Intelligence and an Idea behind everything in this created universe. Recognize that there is tremendous miracle power and vital energy working all the time, and yet there is minute attention to the tiniest details in the plan for all creation. Look around and see the bigness and allness of a miracle project beyond anything the human mind can even begin to conceive, understand or explain.

Let your soul expand in recognition, and open the way for more power to come in to enrich your thinking, your feeling, your awareness and your sense of participation in the great plan of the universe.

Go out of doors on a starry night and try to count the stars. Remember that these shining orbs in the sky, and uncounted others beyond, represent whole galaxies such as ours, and perhaps larger ones as well. Man is only beginning to know his own neighborhood. And how much more there is beyond!

To make the miracle power and the universal plan more personal to you, and to learn from something more your size, bring your consideration down to some small object of God's creation. Study a flower or watch a bird. See the attention to detail and the loving care that went into designing and fashioning even the tiniest feather and petal. And wonder at the miracle of it all.

If God went to so much trouble in clothing the bird and designing the blossom, how much more has he put into designing you and equipping you for life. Recognize this, remember it, open yourself to a greater outpouring of His life, His intelligence and His ideas through you, and you will find that truly you are a spiritual powerhouse—unlimited!

The more you recognize universal power at work, the more you see of the vital energy that is creating and recreating your world and everything in it, the more power you will have flowing in and through your mind, your body and your affairs.

Recognition is a very important part of prayer. It should not contribute to a sense of smallness and insignificance on your part, but should lead you to feel yourself a part of a big miracle, a tremendous plan, a great undertaking. It should give you a sense of identification with mammoth things in the making, and a desire to let more of this universal miracle power find its way through your own personal powerhouse. It should help you to deepen your own desire to make a worth-while contribution to the fulfillment of the over-all plan for universal good. And you can, when your miracle power is turned on!

The more you devote time, thought power, and feeling to the recognition of a Higher Power, the more you will become a channel for the miracle power.

Prayer Generates Miracle Power

Appreciation, too, is necessary in prayer. It constitutes a vital part in releasing spiritual energy in your life.

Appreciation appreciates that which is appreciated, and it works for prayer as for anything else in life.

Appreciate the Power that created you and sustains you in life! Appreciate, instead of depreciating, God's creation. Recognize gratefully His miracle power at work to heal. Recognize gratefully His intelligence now teaching and leading you, even though you don't understand it completely. Recognize, appreciate, and let the spiritual power flow!

Dr. Alexis Carrel, the physician who gained world-wide fame for his investigations of healing at the shrine of Lourdes in France, described prayer as "a force as real as terrestrial gravity." He called it "the most powerful form of energy that one can generate."

And recognition and appreciation are two vital facets of prayer at its best. They are switches that literally release God's power in man's life.

Through prayer you can be healed of any difficulty. God created your body; He can restore it. You can be prospered beyond anything you can even imagine at this present time. You can be guided, even when all human reasoning has failed. You can find an answer to any problem, no matter how hopeless it seems. You can be comforted, when all human comfort has failed. You can be uplifted, energized and inspired to tremendous new activity, even when it means starting all over again. You can expect miracles, and see them happen!

There is a spiritual powerhouse in you now, and there is a power in prayer to turn the switch and let the divine energy pour forth to fill your need, whatever it is.

Recognition and appreciation are only two of the miracle methods that turn on the spiritual power through prayer. There are others, and they will be introduced in the balance of this book.

But before you go farther, here is a warning you will do well to heed:

Spiritual power is truly "the most powerful form of energy that one can generate." It will perform wonders for you when released through you. But with it goes responsibility for using it rightly.

Accept your responsibility, use it only for good, and you will find your life an increasingly wonderful experience. If you try to turn on the miracle power and then dam it up for selfish purposes only, you will suffer terrible consequences of your greed.

But make up your mind to let divine intelligence direct the energy and power you release through spiritual methods, turn your spiritual powerhouse on full, and you will be healthy, prosperous and happy. Not only that, but you will make a vital contribution to the unfoldment of the universal plan of good, you will find joy and satisfaction in doing it, and miracles will happen to you!

Chapter 2

Say Goodbye to Worry, Anxiety and Fear

In order to let the miracle power flow freely through your life, you must keep the channels open. And this means getting rid of many of the states of mind and attitudes toward life that short-circuit the power when it is turned on.

Many of these habits of thinking are deep-seated and tenacious. Even when you are beginning to grasp the concept of the powerhouse within you and trying to use the principles of recognition and appreciation to get yourself up to maximum output in the miracle-power department, you may discover that you have been sidetracked. It can start with a doubt, a fear, an anxious concern about what might happen, even a tremendous feeling of inadequacy and despondency.

Don't worry about it! This is not a defeat, but the beginning of a victory. It is simply the signal that there is something in your mind that needs to be cleared out, so that the power can flow freely and miracles can happen!

A short circuit doesn't mean the end of electric power in your home. It simply indicates that repairs are needed. And so it is in your mind. When you find yourself sidetracked, discouraged or despondent, accept the signal for what it is and clear the obstacle so that your miracle power can come through.

It is never too late to correct a malfunction in the system so that you can operate at full power.

Don't Look into the Cannon's Mouth!

Sometimes clearing the mistake from mind can be as simple as taking this bit of advice:

Don't look into the cannon's mouth!

One beautiful September day I was enjoying the view from Edinburgh Castle in Scotland. I sat high on the ramparts and looked out across picturesque rooftops of the new town to the dark blue water of the Firth of Forth in the distance.

It was a clear, crisp day, and I enjoyed the day and the view for some time before I became aware of the groups of tourists pausing near me. Then I discovered that each time a tour conductor brought his group past where I sat, he called their attention to a huge cannon pointing out toward the Firth.

He told how large the gun was, how far it would shoot, and gave other information pertinent to guns. When he finished, each tourist obediently walked over to look into the cannon's mouth before continuing the tour. Only an occasional tourist glanced at the beauty of the panoramic view before the group moved on to the next point of interest.

After a while I began to wonder what they found so fascinating in the cannon's mouth, and I, too, walked over to look. There was nothing there but a lot of darkness and a few bits of trash left by earlier visitors.

As I turned back to the panorama of beauty beyond the castle walls, I thought, "How many people spend their lives looking into the mouth of destructive elements, contemplating their power to harm! How many people fail to lift their eyes and see the beauty all around them!"

You look into the cannon's mouth every time you bury yourself in thoughts of your problems or difficulties. You look into the cannon's mouth every time you anticipate all of the bad things that can happen under certain circumstances. You look into the cannon's mouth every time you involve yourself, mentally and emotionally, in contemplation of destructive elements.

Miracle power may be all around you. It may be on the verge

of breaking through and flooding your life with good. But it can't come forth until you break your absorption with problems and difficulties, recognize that the good is there, and invite it into your life!

Concentration Concentrates the Problem

There is a law of concentration, and it is this:

That which receives your concentrated attention will be concentrated in your life.

If you concentrate on your feelings of inadequacy, you will become increasingly less able to handle life. If you worry about the possibility of loss, you increase the losses in your life. If you believe in lack and give it your undivided attention for a period of time, you will find that limitation spreads through other areas of your life as well. If you worry about conditions, fear that they will become worse, and concentrate the power of your thought and feeling on things you don't like and would like to see changed, they will simply become worse than ever.

Worry never solved a problem. Anxious concentration never brought a solution. And the very act of concentrating on that which is wrong, that which has been wrong, or that which may be wrong concentrates and increases the difficulty that caused your concern in the first place.

Many times people feel that, by concentrating on the error, they will solve it. But it just doesn't work this way. To remove an error, you must concentrate on a solution, never on the difficulty itself.

You have all of the miracle power you can ever use available to help you remove stumbling blocks, as well as to increase good in every department of life and living. But not one bit of the power can get through when you set up a block of concentrating all of your energies on the things that are wrong in your life—even when you are just wondering why they happened to you.

There is a law of concentration, and it works both ways. If you want to reap the benefits of the right working of this law in your life, you must co-operate with it by concentrating only on those things which you want to see increased.

This isn't always easy. Most people have formed the habit of giving their undivided attention to problems and difficulties. In a sense, modern society is more at home with its problems than with its potentiality. A great deal more is written about the things that are wrong in the world than about those things which are right and can be better.

Concentration concentrates the thing on which it is focused. A change in the direction of concentration can turn on the miracle power to correct those things which are wrong.

Break the Spell

But can you break the spell? Can you stop worrying and start believing in good? Can you give up your thoughts of gloom and despondency long enough to decide that things can get better? Can you even get rid of those little doubts and fears, that persistent feeling of inadequacy, long enough to open the way for the miracle power to help you?

You can if you want to—badly enough to determine to succeed, and to work at it until you do.

Many times when I tell people they must change their habits of thought and free themselves from the feelings that are literally destroying their lives, they answer, "But I can't help thinking about it! I can't help worrying!"

They're looking directly into the mouth of the cannon and saying, "I have to! For me the view doesn't exist."

But the view does exist. The beauty and the goodness are there, wherever you are and whatever you are doing. And miracle power is available to you to help you discover it. But first you must take your head from the mouth of the cannon!

You wouldn't leave your head in a lion's mouth, would you? And yet you are in even greater danger when you continue to bury your thoughts in the contemplation of problems and difficulties and the possibilities of greater problems and greater difficulties.

Desire to look up and look out, and you will do it! Desire it enough to stop saying "I can't" and start saying "I can," and all the miracle power you can use will come to help you do it.

Miracle power is yours for the asking, but it can't get through until you open the way. And you open the way by trusting in it enough to stop believing, even for a moment, in the things that appear to be wrong in your life.

If you will concentrate on beauty and goodness, miracle power finds an open channel and pours itself out as more and more beauty and goodness. But if you insist on concentrating on the destructive power of your own particular cannon, the law works in reverse—and you are the victim of your own weapon.

Worry in Reverse!

Even the word "worry" indicates concentration.

Consider the way a dog worries a bone. He grabs it, shakes it, jerks it, plays with it, mangles it, mauls it and generally gives it his full and undivided attention until he tires of it.

This is what you do when you worry. You take something that has happened or even something that may happen—generally an experience or possibility of a destructive or negative character. Then you think about it. You chew it over in your mind. You pick it up and throw it about, examine it from all angles, and play with the possibilities of even greater danger or difficulty. And the more you worry your bone of a problem, the bigger it gets—until you may say, and believe, "I can't help worrying about it!" But you can. Try the same technique in reverse.

Instead of tossing about the negative aspects of the affair, start thinking of some of the things that are right. There is beauty all around you, if you will simply lift your vision and look at it. Play with the possibilities of good results. Chew the constructive lines of action you can take. Give your full and undivided attention to believing that there is a power which can work miracles in your life when you turn on your personal powerhouse and let it come through.

The moment you completely break the mental tie with whatever has worried you and give the same concentrated attention to the possibility of success, prosperity and health, you have reversed the trend of the law, and you have released your power for miracles.

When you believe in miracles, and concentrate all the intensity of your thought and feeling on good, you not only are freed from the difficulty, but you are better off than you have ever been in your life! Then go back and give thanks for the worry that helped you discover the miracle power in the first place. Give thanks, and release it forever!

Whistle—Don't Scream!

The principle of concentration also works in overcoming fear. Fear is simply a matter of misplaced faith in the first place, and concentration only serves to increase it.

Somewhere I ran across a little modern motto that went like this: "It is better to whistle past the graveyard than to shut one's eyes and scream."

This is true, and it is a good illustration of the idea of attention.

It is better to make an effort to profess courage than to simply give in to fear and let it monopolize your thoughts and actions. And, believe it or not, the more fearless you act, the more fearless you become!

Take the simple example of the graveyard. You can easily see that if you allowed fear to fill your mind so strongly, to become so concentrated in action, that you screamed, the feeling of fear would be increased.

You would feel the scream rising in your throat, and you would identify even more strongly with the fear that prompted it. You would feel all of the physical reactions that are a part of a strong emotional outburst. And, finally, you would hear the scream as it came out and be even more afraid, almost as though it came from someone else.

On the other hand, even though you do feel fright, you will discover that you can retain control over it if you will concentrate on expressing courage. Even though you don't really feel courageous, you can whistle, and concentrate the power of your attention, not on the thing which you fear, but on the simple matter of whistling.

Don't even bother to tell yourself that you aren't afraid. This returns your thought to the feeling of fear. Just give your full and undivided attention to whatever you choose to do to take your attention away from the problem.

Whistle. Sing a song. Play some silly child's game of saying a rhyme in time to your steps. Choose your own release, and then give all the power of your concentrated attention to doing it. Become so busy building courage that you forget to be afraid. The law of concentration will work to diminish the size of the thing you fear and to increase the size of your courage. It's all in your mind, anyway, and it is there that the fear must be met and conquered in the long run. It is there that you must start your overcoming.

Bring the thing you fear, and your emotional reaction to it, down to a size you can handle, and you'll know how to turn on the miracle power to dissolve the whole situation.

Act Like a Hero

You may not feel like a hero, but you can act like one. And when you act like one, pretty soon you begin to create the role.

Whistle if that helps you. March in time to words of courage. Go ahead with what you are doing as though nothing could hurt or harm you anyway. Or concentrate on filling your mind with love, until whatever seems to be an enemy becomes a friend. The main thing is to remember the law of concentration and to work with it in the direction in which you want to go—to freedom.

Courage may not come full-grown to start with, but it does grow. It is increased as you feed it. And the food it requires is rightly directed concentration in thought, word and action.

Never concentrate the fear power by being ashamed of feeling afraid. (Most people at one time or another have occasion to be afraid—even those who never show it.) Instead, give your attention to those methods which work best for you, and build your courage through concentration on them. If you start soon enough, the fear never does grow very big, and when you glance back at it, you'll see that the miracle power has worked to dissolve it entirely.

When you recognize a danger signal, turn on the neutralizer. Instead of giving in to terror, "whistle past the graveyard," sing while you pray, or work while you wait. You'll find the remedy that works best for you, and, when you do, you will be able to conquer fear every time.

It doesn't really matter what is the cause of your fright or apprehensiveness. The fear itself is in you, and it is here that it must be corrected. You can't afford to be afraid, because fear plugs up the outlet for the miracle power in your life.

The graveyard in your particular experience may be fear that is based on dead hopes, buried talents or present prospects that show no signs of life or growth. It can be caused by anything from a disease or physical problem to the actual threat of another person. The cause isn't important when you have found the cure.

Put all the power of concentration to work for you in building courage, and you will see that the miracle power has somehow cured the fear. And, when it has, then you are ready to face and handle the situation that caused the fear in the first place.

You are ready for the miracle of true freedom! All you have to do is let it happen through you.

Don't Say It, Unless You Want It

You may intensify fear, anxiety, worry and the situations which cause them through your words. Here, again, that which is concentrated in the spoken word becomes increased.

Sometimes the effect of your words is readily seen, but in other cases the result may be so subtle that you never even connect it with the cause. But the words you speak have greater strength to increase worry and fear than even your thoughts about them.

In order to put your fears and concerns into words, you must really intensify them in thought. To choose the words to describe a difficulty, you have to think about it, around it and through it. You test first one sentence and then another, in your mind, seeking to find the one that best describes your feeling. And then, finally, you say it. Besides all the power of concentration that is working in the words, you have the added emphasis of the thoughts behind them.

Don't put into words anything you don't want to see expressed in life! Never say you are afraid a certain thing will happen—unless, of course, you want it to. Never tell how worried you are about other

persons or particular situations. The worry expressed in words is
even stronger than the worry in your mind.

"How Are You?"

Even when someone asks "How are you?" you can use the miracle
power of concentration to improve your mental attitude, your health
and your circumstances.

Your words concentrate your thoughts and feelings. What do they
tell about you, even in a simple matter such as answering a common
greeting?

Maybe you have answered, as many people do, with a reply
designed to sound not too well, too happy or too well-satisfied with
life in general. Some people seem to feel that they really shouldn't
be too cheerful about it all. And so they answer "Pretty well" or
"As well as can be expected."

And for years they remain just that—"pretty well" or "as well
as can be expected," in a worried, anxious state of mind. They stay
in the rut of not too well, not too happy and not too well-satisfied
with life in general, when they could be living joyously with a
full, free flow of miracle power working for them night and day.

Or perhaps you are like those persons who take the simple question "How are you?" as a personal project. They examine themselves
mentally, physically and emotionally before making a reply. And by
the time they finish, they are ready to detail a great many things
that are wrong with the state of their lives.

When you look long enough and hard enough, you can always
find some ache or pain to describe, some problem with other persons,
perhaps members of your family—or at least a little negative story
that can be developed into a conversation piece.

If you fall into the category of those who automatically answer
the question "Just fine!" then you are already working to become
just fine. And that is good, whether or not you are aware of what
you are doing. It doesn't hurt to say words that express what you
want to be, even when you speak them automatically and scarcely
notice what you are saying.

"Filled with the Joy of Living"

I know one person who answers the question with this reply: "I am filled with the joy of living." And he is. Claiming something like this is a good way to whistle past any graveyard of worry or fear. It is a good method for overcoming any tendency to analyze and detail illnesses or difficulties.

Just saying "I am filled with the joy of living" turns on the miracle power. Try it, and see.

Choose a positive answer that suits your particular requirements, and then say it. Maybe you'd like to claim, "I'm fine now, and getting better all the time."

Sometimes people ask, "How can I say I'm fine when I don't feel fine?"

Say it, believe it, concentrate on it, and it will become true for you. This is the way the miracle power works.

In a class on spiritual principles, I suggested that all of us say together, with joy and enthusiasm, "I am radiant with life and vitality."

After we had repeated the statement three times, we had generated such a strong feeling of life and vitality that every face in the room showed it.

Undoubtedly there were those who had come into the room with some worry or concern in their minds, but they left with a feeling of life and vitality and an ability to face whatever needed to be handled in their lives.

This is the way the power of concentration works to get rid of fear, worry and anxiety. And when you are free of the thought and the feeling, when you no longer emphasize it by your words, when you have learned to "whistle past the graveyard," then you are ready to turn on the miracle power and let it pour forth to establish life, vitality—the joy of living, all of the good that you can ever use.

Miracles happen to the one who opens the channel and lets the power flow!

Chapter 3

Put Yourself in the Picture

Miracle power! It can do wonderful things through you. But, to put it to work in your life, you must make it real and personal to you.

You are reading about it. It sounds good, and you would like to use it to change your life. You relate to it to a certain degree. You begin opening the channels for it to flow through, using the principles of recognition, appreciation and concentration. Now connect it specifically to yourself and your aims in life.

Use the miracle power to draw a new sketch of yourself, your abilities, your talents, and the entire direction of your life. Use the miracle power to create a whole new picture of what you can be like, what you essentially are like in your highest nature, and what life can be like for you. Then put yourself in the picture!

Don't be content to be a mediocre person living a mediocre existence and satisfied with mediocre aims in life. You were designed to be something special, and you were given all the equipment, including your own built-in powerhouse, to do great things! Aim toward those things, and you will get there.

Choose a Goal

Many times people complain that they aren't getting anywhere. They explain that they go to work, come home, do certain things they are accustomed to doing at certain times, go to bed, sleep awhile, get up, and start all over. They sum up their lives by saying, "I'm not getting anywhere."

If this ever happens to you, and you feel that your life has become a pointless existence, stop and ask yourself, "But where do I want to go?" As a matter of fact, you might ask yourself this question anyway.

Where do you want to go? Do you have any clear idea?

The principle of direction is this:

If you aren't giving direction to your life, consciously and creatively, you will fall into the rut of not getting anywhere. There is nowhere to go until you choose a goal.

All too many people have no idea where they would like to go in life. They have never chosen any realistic basic goals, and they go through a certain number of years drifting, instead of directed.

You don't have to do this. You can choose your goal and learn to identify with it, so that life can be a continuing adventure in living for you.

By identifying with your goal I mean making it real to you, establishing it as something that is not only a possibility but already part of you in your mind and in your feeling nature, something that is yours by right of your mental claim.

You don't have to choose a tremendous goal to begin with. Let the larger aims wait until you have learned the technique that releases miracle power in your mind and in your affairs. Selecting smaller aims and reaching them serves to build confidence and trust in the miracle power and in your own ability to receive and use it.

Choose a goal that is realistic, based on your present position, but choose one that will test your faith and your sincerity at least a little—something that, at first, you aren't quite sure you can achieve, something you really would like to do but somehow have never had the courage to try.

It can be something as simple as making a telephone call and contacting a new friend, or joining an evening class in some subject you have always wanted to study.

I know a woman who chose a goal of improving her bowling

game, and she did, so spectacularly that her friends could scarcely believe it.

Choose your own goal. You are the only one who can determine what you want from life, because you are the only one who lives inside your particular self.

Guideposts Within

But inside that self you will find many guideposts to the attaining of worth-while aims in life.

What are the goals you truly would like to attain? What are those areas you have always wished to explore, but never had the courage to do so? What interests you? What dreams do you have when you let your imagination carry you into new and wonderful worlds?

Your desires, your hopes and your dreams are guideposts to the things you can achieve and the self you can become, at this particular time in your life. Only you can see them, because they are inside you. And so you must choose for yourself.

Let the miracle power help you. Let this new awareness lead you, mentally and spiritually, into a new picture of yourself, a new sense of direction, and new aims and goals for living.

Relax, and let the picture unfold in your mind. Let it take shape and begin to assume outlines and direction. When you open yourself to inner guidance, your own miracle power flows in to form an image of the goals and aims that you can best achieve at the present time.

The miracle power itself pours into your mind in the form of new ideas, new concepts, new possibilities you would like to explore, new pictures, new aims, and new roads to be followed. Sometimes they will be quite clear and definite. At other times the images may seem obscure. But they will come when you open the way by pointing your thoughts in the direction of choosing a goal, and then let the inner power help you define it.

Those guideposts which you discover within yourself at this particular time are only the beginning of the way you can travel when you turn on the miracle power and let it lead you forward.

There are potentialities and possibilities in the realm of Spirit that are far beyond man's present ability to imagine. But they will be shown to you and expressed through you as you increase your ability to receive and express the vision.

There is a divine plan for the whole universe. Nothing happens by chance. All nature grows, and all actions and reactions are governed by a predetermined network of laws and plans by which every form of life expresses itself.

There is a plan for your life. This is not a predestined path you must take, but it is, rather, a plan of such magnitude that only in your highest awareness of your potential can you even begin to grasp its significance for you. But this plan holds within it many potentialities for your advancement at the present time. And, when you put yourself into the picture of the good you can desire and envision now, you open the way for the greater revelation of what life can be like for you.

Everything that ever was, is, or can be, exists already as an idea in the mind that created the universe and set this vast mechanism into operation. Some people call this reservoir Divine Mind; some refer to it as universal mind; others say God. But all who have investigated the laws of the universe to even the smallest degree must admit that there is a vast plan by which all facets of existence are governed. It is only slightly understood at the present time, but it is evident to anyone who searches for greater truths, whether in spiritual realms or in scientific laboratories.

When you turn on the miracle power in your mind, seeking to choose those goals and aims which are right for your life at this particular time, you are literally tuning into the highest and greatest plan for your life, the one that already exists in Divine Mind.

You won't be able to see all the possibilities, but you will be able to see some. If you can grasp even a little of the plan that is there to be fulfilled by you, if you can begin to work with even a few of these miracle methods, if you can learn how to bring these ideas alive in your experience, then you are on your way to the expression of greater and greater miracle power, to the fulfillment of your highest aims and hopes—and to goals even beyond these!

The more you work with this power, and the more you learn to

release it as needed, the more sure you will be of the plan as it un-
folds for you, and the more easily you will fit, and grow, into it.

Start Where You Are

Start where you are. Choose a goal that appeals to you particularly
at the present time, one that is just a little beyond your present
abilities, one that you really want to achieve. Then go to work on it.

It is not enough to dream, to think, to wish. You must believe
it can be so. You must put yourself in the picture—mentally and
spiritually first, and finally physically. You must learn to identify
with it, to see yourself doing it, being it, living it. You must become
so much a part of the plan mentally and emotionally that you have
to fit into it physically.

You do this by working with the law of vision, which is this:

Whatever you can see yourself doing, you can do! Whatever you
can see yourself being, you can be! Whatever you can see yourself
achieving, you can achieve!

This is not a new method. Many people have used it through
the years. But it does work for anyone who is willing to give himself
up to making it work for him.

You can be completely and beautifully healthy, vitally alive. But
you will never be strong and well until you are able to picture
yourself that way. In order to have this goal fulfilled, you must put
yourself in the picture of health, life, joy and vigor.

You can be completely and joyously happy in your work. But in
order to accomplish this, you must stop feeling sorry for yourself
when others impose on you. You have to give up remembrance of
the difficulties, and the reasons why your job isn't satisfactory. Instead, you must picture yourself doing a good job, doing it with joy
and ease, and being successful in it.

You can be successful in your dealings with other persons. But
here, again, the key is in your vision. In order to get along with
others, you have to stop waiting for them to change, and start
changing yourself. Do it first in your mind, by picturing yourself
the way you want to be in all your dealings with others, poised, relaxed, smiling, happy, peaceful and harmonious at all times. Catch

the vision of the person you want to be, and you become that person. The miracle power just works that way.

You can attain any pinnacle for which you aim—when you can see yourself doing it.

Retouch the Photograph

When you visit a professional photographer, you expect something special from him. You want a picture which will look just a little better than you do. You'd like for it to be recognizable, but you certainly don't expect him to leave in the finished photo the lines and defects you would rather forget. If you don't like the photograph, you blame the photographer, most likely.

But what if you don't like the mental photograph you have of yourself? Suppose you find it difficult to reconcile this person you see in your mind with the one who is necessary to fulfill those aims and goals you have chosen for yourself.

Then blame the photographer! You are the one who is producing the picture, and you have the power to retouch it and remove those blemishes which will keep you, physically, mentally or emotionally, from fitting into the greater photograph of yourself.

You must revamp this picture through the power of your imagination if you are to fit into the unfolding plan of good for your life. And you can use the miracle power to do it!

Don't hesitate to claim greater things for yourself, and to do it in your mental picturing of the person you really are. This is not vanity, and it is not idle dreaming. Rightly done, it is constructive preparation for the person you want to become, and it is a necessary part of becoming that person.

You will never be healthier until the picture in your mind shows health, not weakness and illness. You will never be richer until the picture in your mind shows one living in abundance, not existing in lack. You will never be more talented until the picture in your mind shows great accomplishments, not reasons why they can't be done.

Retouching your mental photograph is a matter of removing from your thoughts all of the limitations that would hamper your forward progress, and replacing them with positive images that express the qualities you will need in order to achieve your goals. Then you can develop the photograph through your words and actions. Stand up and speak up! Be your best self. You can do it when you can picture yourself doing it!

What Can You Do?

This may not be easy. It may take some real, uphill work on your part, but when you put forth your best efforts, the miracle power rushes in to help you achieve your aim.

One day I was talking to a friend who had been through many physical difficulties. She was telling me her problems and detailing the things she couldn't do because of her present condition.

Since she had asked for my help, I stopped her and asked, "What can you do?"

She looked at me in surprise. But because she was an intelligent woman and really did want to help herself, she stopped and considered the question seriously. As she thought about it, she realized that there were a great many things that she could do, but she had been so busy building the picture of her difficulties that she had forgotten them. She had set the limitations so squarely in the middle of the photograph of herself that there was no room for the possibilities and potentialities she could develop.

Seeing her error, she determined to concentrate on the things she could do. Then, as she looked at some of the areas where she had felt that the situation was hopeless, she realized that even there she could do much more than she had been doing. Perhaps she couldn't see as well as she would like to see, but she could see somewhat. And she determined to stop talking about her sight in a derogatory manner and use the sight she had.

She gained more than physical sight by that decision. She also gained a new spiritual insight and set the wheels in motion for her continued improvement. When she began to develop her spiritual vision and to put herself in the picture, through the right focusing of her built-in camera, she changed her life immediately.

And so can you. The law works, but only you can make it work for you.

No matter how much spiritual power is waiting to be expressed in your life, to heal, to harmonize, to strengthen, to prosper, it can't come in until you open the way. And you turn the switch and let it flow when you faithfully and positively work with the law of vision.

Whatever you can see yourself doing, you can do! Whatever you can see yourself being, you can be! Whatever you can see yourself achieving, you can achieve!

But the law also works this way:

Whatever you see yourself as unable to do, you can't do! Whatever you see limiting you, will continue to limit your expression of good. And whatever you set squarely in the middle of your mental photograph as a handicap, will be just that.

Retouch the picture in your mind. Remove those unsightly scars in your thinking. Cover up the blemishes by determining to work from a higher understanding and a greater purpose in the future. It is to your advantage to make that mental photograph everything that you want to be, because the law is even now working to express what you are seeing in your mind.

The Vision of Champions

Even great opportunities may be passed up when you refuse to put yourself in the picture of what you want to be, what you truly desire to attain.

In the Masters Golf Tournament, held in the spring of 1965 at Augusta, Georgia, one of the golfers surprised the gallery with a remarkably low score for the qualifying round. Soon he was being hailed as a favorite to win.

But he told reporters, "I can't see myself winning the tournament; it will be one of the big boys, like Nicklaus."

Sure enough, Jack Nicklaus was the winner.

Champions are always people who have been able to catch the vision, the inner picture, of themselves winning—the race, the tournament, and even the game of life.

Miracle power works in a tremendous way for those who let it come in, whether or not they recognize what they are doing at the time.

It is always interesting to read about the preparations champions in the athletic fields go through to become winners. Many of them speak of mentally negotiating the course or running the race, with emphasis on the correct technique for each turn. In addition to going through the physical training that is necessary, they must prepare themselves mentally to be winners. Otherwise, even at the last moment, something can go wrong to take them out of the race. But when they put themselves in the picture of success and do the work that is necessary to back up the ideal, sooner or later they are bound to come in first.

And so it is with you.

See yourself a winner! You may not want to enter the Olympics, but you are already entered in the greatest game of all—the game of life. Learn to make the most of it by sketching the champion you would like to be, and putting yourself in the picture.

You can overcome whatever obstacles lie in your way. You can climb higher, live longer, be richer, or do anything in the championship class that you choose to be or do. But first you must catch the vision of yourself doing it, being it, experiencing it.

If you will let the miracle power within help you to choose and shape the goal in your mind, you will be not only successful and happy in one particular field, but successful and happy in living. And this is a worth-while goal for any person.

Miracle power will enable you to formulate the right and perfect goal in the first place, the one that is appropriate for you at this particular time. Miracle power will help you to put yourself in the picture. And miracle power will help you get there. This is the law of vision.

Chapter 4

Succeed by Doing

Once you have caught the vision, once you have put yourself in the picture of success, achievement, being and doing, you are ready to apply another law in making the miracle power work for you.

You can be and do anything. You can achieve goals beyond your greatest imagining at this present time. By now you have chosen some aims with which you can identify, and you are ready to move toward them in your life.

Miracle power will not do all the work for you! Miracle power will not do for you those things which you are unwilling to do for yourself! Miracle power is not a magic amulet to be used instead of muscle power. It is, rather, the extra, added impetus toward success that does for you those things which you are not able to do for yourself.

Miracle power will not work in spite of you, but it will work with you! It will not force good on you, but it will help you when you are engaged in the search for something better and greater in your life.

It is the activity which was described by a Man who had learned to work with it to perform works above and beyond the understanding of the human mind. Jesus Christ put it this way: "With men it is impossible, but not with God: for with God all things are possible." (Mark 10:27 KJV)

In the realm of human understanding, many things simply are not possible, but when you are willing to awaken the miracle power within yourself, and do all that is humanly possible, the Power itself takes over and does the rest. Nothing is impossible to the miracle power, because it operates on higher laws and greater understanding. But it works with anyone who is willing to use it for good.

Desire Makes the Difference

Wishing won't make it so, no matter how much you give yourself to dreaming dreams and wishing for things that have never been. But desiring will accomplish all things through you.

The difference is this. When you simply wish for something, you take it out in idle thinking. But when you truly desire to be, to do or to have something new and wonderful, you are willing to act! Not only do you have the vision and the identification with it, but you also have the impetus that pushes you into action, into doing those things which you can do to bring it about.

This is the principle of action:

You can't do everything, perhaps, but you can do something! Those things which you can't do, miracle power can and will accomplish for you, when you take the first steps. Not only that, but once you are under way, miracle power flows in to give you increased strength, added understanding and greater abilities. The things you can do when you have finished the job are greater than the talents and abilities with which you started the project.

Wishing won't make it so, but desiring will, because desire leads to action.

Action alone is not enough. Without proper stimulus and direction, it becomes aimless and perhaps even desperate. But with desire, aim and vision, action, directed by miracle power, leads to success!

Desire adds something else to the direction of activity. It adds a determination to reach the goal that is chosen. And this is necessary to successful living.

It is easy to think of reasons why something can't be done, or can't be done by you. But when you are sparked by a determination, a deep-down desire, you refuse to consider the reasons why you should fail, but rather concentrate on the methods that will carry you to achievement.

Well-defined goals, visualized in mind and backed up by a strong desire, lead to the right kind of action for ultimate triumph. This is the law, and it works!

Don't Try—Do It!

Desire doesn't stop with trying. It doesn't even consider the possibility of failure but identifies with success and thus calls the miracle power into action to make it so. Desire separates the daydreams from the real aims and goals of your life.

Recently I overheard an employer giving instructions to a woman employee.

When he finished, she said doubtfully, "Well, I'll try."

His answer was quick and decisive:

"Don't try—do it!"

And this is the instruction that desire gives.

It is also the principle of desire:

Desire isn't willing to compromise with a noble effort. It doesn't stop with just trying. It does the thing toward which it is directed, because it believes that it can be, and must be, done.

This is the impetus that propels you toward the fulfillment of your aims and goals, your new vision of yourself. This is that in you which awakens even greater activity of the miracle power, and the miracle power is unlimited!

Miracle power can make you an accomplished musician, a great speaker, an inspired writer or just a happy, well-adjusted person. But in each case there is work to be done by you, and it must be done with willingness to invest time and effort, and with the expectation of success.

A young girl approached Marian Anderson, the well-known singer, after a concert. She was filled with the inspiration of the music as she said, "I'd give anything in the world if I could sing like that!"

Miss Anderson looked at her searchingly and asked, "Would you give eight hours of practice a day?"

Stars in your eyes are not enough to achieve any worth-while goal in life. But stars in your eyes and desire in your heart lead to action, action with the full expectation of success, and purposeful, rightly directed action leads to the achievement of your highest aims and goals.

Any aim in life that is worth choosing is worth working for.

Success that is gained through short cuts or what is called luck can be lost as easily as it is won. The fame that comes quickly may leave as suddenly. Riches gained without effort may be lost in a moment.

But goals reached through deep-down desire and effort, those backed up and enforced by the activity of miracle power, are yours forever.

Bring the Project Down to Size

Sometimes at first glance the task ahead may seem tremendous, almost too much to attempt. But miracle power has the ability to diminish the size of the task as it increases your faith and confidence.

You can overcome any condition or make a success of any new undertaking when you have, deep within yourself, the conviction that the job can be completed, and that it can be done by you!

It doesn't help just to believe that someone else can do it. You must build the conviction within yourself that you can fit into the picture of health, success and accomplishment that you have outlined in your mind. This must be the deep-down conviction that you can do it—not that someone else could, but that you yourself can reach the goal you have chosen! And you can use miracle power to help you build this inner knowing and faith.

Release the power in your mind and in your feelings by identifying with it mentally and emotionally. Say to yourself, "I believe it can be done, and with the help of the miracle power in me, I can do it!"

Perhaps you can't do it in a personal, limited way, but that is not the point. With miracle power, you are unlimited! Impress this on your mind and on your emotions until you are so sure that there is no more doubt at all. And you are ready to do whatever needs to be done by you.

At first, when you say, "I believe it can be done, and with the help of the miracle power in me, I can do it!" you may not even believe that it can be done in the first place. But anything you can visualize completely in your mind, anything that you truly desire to express in your life, you can bring forth.

Say these words over and over. Give time and attention to thinking about your particular, chosen project, associating in your mind with the picture of yourself doing it. Keep telling yourself that it can be done, and you can do it by opening the way for the miracle power to work.

If you want your thought to be even stronger, put it this way: "I believe it can be done, and God can do it through me." God can do tremendous things through you. Actually, the miracle power is God in action. But using the word "God" gives increased power to your thought.

With miracle power working through you, you are well on your way to success. But with God acknowledged as the directing power in your life, you are just beginning a great unfolding adventure of life and growth, one that is beyond your grandest imagining at the present time.

When you have convinced yourself that the project you have chosen can be done, and that it can be done by you, with the help of God, or miracle power, then go ahead and do it!

People have a way of talking themselves out of attempting certain things by considering the reasons why their plan won't work. But you don't even have to consider such points when you are working with miracle power. As a matter of fact, you can't afford to, because concepts of limitation take your attention away from the energy you need in order to accomplish.

Don't even think about possibilities of failure. Outline the plan, let it take shape in your mind, and then go to work and do it!

Enlarge the Channel

Even if you don't see results as quickly as you had hoped, don't allow yourself to go back to those thoughts of limitation and failure. Anything worth while takes time and patience, faith and persistence, even with miracle power flowing through. The activity of this power will speed up the results, but it can only express itself if you allow it to come through. Remember, it is flowing through the confined area of your present understanding and ability, and understanding and talent must be developed and enlarged to let more come into your life.

Miracle power can only work in your life through you. It will not circumvent your own channel in order to express itself in spite of you. It comes clearly and definitely into your life through the channel you provide for it within yourself. If you aren't satisfied with the present flow of miracle power, if you don't see immediate results, then don't give up. Work on enlarging the inlet and the outlet.

You wouldn't condemn a ditch that became clogged and only allowed a trickle of water to come through; you would get a shovel and go to work to open it up, and that's what you must do to enable your own particular powerhouse to operate at full capacity— keep working until you open the way for an increased flow of power. It is there, but you have to prepare to receive and to use it.

If your desire is to become a great artist, you won't expect to have a one-man show the first month. You will be willing to practice, to develop your talent in an orderly way, and finally to express, through art, what you want to express. Even the matter of developing a particular technique, one that is peculiarly yours, takes time.

If you would like to be successful in business, don't become discouraged if customers don't beat a path to your door the first week, the first month, or even the first year. Study the needs of those whom you would like to serve, go forward in faith, implementing your business in any way that seems advisable in the light of your growing understanding, and get ready for greater success to come.

Be willing to take the steps of training that are necessary. These, too, are a part of the principle of action. Be willing to learn. Be ready for new ideas. Be willing to experiment with new methods. Desire to render service and to give good to others as a part of your undertaking. Be willing to work, in order to earn the right to success, and you will have success beyond your present ability to imagine.

All of the great men of history have at some time or another proved their ability to do small things well, before going on to the greater place of service that life offered them.

Johann Friedrich von Schiller, the great German dramatist of the eighteenth century, once said, "Only those who have the patience to do simple things perfectly will acquire the skill to do difficult things easily."

This is true even when you are working with miracle power. The inner flow of this vital energy and knowing will make the work easier and increase your abilities, but you must still be willing to serve your apprenticeship as you learn.

Don't Take It Out in Talking

Having been a professional writer, I am occasionally introduced to would-be writers. Frequently these people tell me at great length about the books they intend to write some day, when they have more time. But when I ask what other writing they are doing, they look at me in surprise. They simply think in terms of someday writing a great novel or a best-selling autobiography. Their thinking is not backed up by desire. It is simply idle daydreaming, something that sounds pretty good in conversation.

One who desires to write will be willing to learn and to practice. He will have the desire that leads to action, and will not content himself with talking about what he wants to do.

As a matter of fact, you will discover that when you start to work toward your chosen goal, you will make more progress if you don't do a great deal of talking about what you want to accomplish.

Talk uses energy. Sometimes it requires so much energy to tell others about the project that you simply don't have any left to accomplish the work.

Idle conversation dissipates the power in your mind and in your body, letting it escape without accomplishing anything constructive, and this is a waste that you can't afford if you are determined to reach the goals you have set for yourself.

Using energy and vitality to outline your project and your aims, mentally, is a good investment. But just talking about what you want to do will not get you where you want to go. Your next investment should be in rightly directed action, activity that is outlined in mind by the miracle power working in your thinking and feeling nature.

Build your inner picture, act as you are shown the way, and stick with your project through those early days of practice and patience. Do this, and you will achieve your goal, at the right time and in the right way, when you have prepared the way.

You don't have to do everything, but you must do something. You don't have to do those things which are impossible for you, but you have to prepare the channel for the miracle power to flow through in order to do them.

Finish It!

Don't try to name the time that you should see results. In order to judge the progress you are making, you must take your mind away from the goal you are seeking. So don't do it. Just keep your inner vision on the goal, keep going, and you'll get there when everything is right, and you are ready.

Sometimes people try for a certain length of time, and then, thinking they haven't accomplished all that they should have done, they stop in discouragement.

If you ever find yourself ready to give up, stop and consider this point:

If you stop trying before you reach your goal, you will never know how close you came to it! There is only one way to find out how near you are to reaching it, and that is to keep going until you get there.

If you stop before the race is finished, you never know how close you came to winning. If you give up because something seems difficult, or even impossible, you may not discover how close you came to making a break-through.

Persistence is a key to success in anything, and sometimes an ounce of persistence spells the difference between complete success and dismal failure. You never know how close you are to achieving the thing you want to do, until you persist that little extra bit and finish. If it is worth undertaking in the first place, it is worth finishing!

The last hour may be the hardest, but it is the most worth while, after all, because it brings the reward of all those hours that went before.

The joy of finishing a difficult job more than repays the effort of that last inch, for at least two reasons.

First of all, when you finish one job and see it work out well, you have a greater incentive and a stronger faith to tackle the next piece of work and see it through. There is no reward quite so worth while as the feeling of having completed a difficult job and done it well. This is worth all the effort and persistence.

Second, finishing one job helps you to build a habit of persisting to the end. It also does something for your mental attitude in general.

To a large degree, your life is based on habits. When you form the habit of stopping short of your goal, this is a custom that will make it easy to give up the next time. But when you form the habit of seeing things through, this becomes easier each time you do it.

It is simply good mental training to make yourself finish, particularly when you have decided that you would rather not, or that it probably won't work anyway.

If you can start, you can finish. And if you need a little more energy and faith to see you through those last few miles of the road, go back and reconstruct your vision with the words you used earlier: "I believe it can be done, and with the help of the miracle power in me, I can do it!" Or make it even stronger by declaring, "I believe the job can be finished, and God can do it through me." Then let Him.

This is a principle that works, and it will work for you.

Develop a deep-down desire to reach a particular goal, build the picture in your mind, take the action that is necessary for you, and miracle power will do the rest. When you work with miracle power, you can succeed in every worth-while undertaking, by doing your part!

Chapter 5

Strike Oil in Unexpected Places

Miracles will happen in your life when you learn to work with miracle power. But don't be surprised if other things happen as well.

Sometimes when people begin to work with this power, they are so thrilled with the results that they are sure they will never have problems again. This is not so.

There are many ways in which your good can come to you, many ways in which you can bring in the oil wells of riches beyond your grandest dreams. And, believe it or not, some of these opportunities are waiting for you now in the guise of what you call problems.

Stop calling them problems, disappointments, failures, frustrations and misfortunes. Rename them challenges, dares, that life presents to call forth your noblest efforts. Each challenge met and overcome provides its own recompense of good, and the greater the challenge at the time, the greater the reward it brings. Challenges are teachers, when you are willing to learn the lesson they bring, and they are opportunities as well.

Working with miracle power does not guarantee that you will never have challenges to meet, but it does guarantee you the know-how and wherewithal to meet them and come out victorious. No matter how dark the situation you face, no matter how great the challenge, there is a reward inherent in the experience itself, and a working knowledge of miracle power will speed you on your way to claim it.

You can, and will, strike oil in the most unexpected places when you let the miracle power help you find the blessing in every challenge that comes.

No One Can Hold You Back

Most people meet challenges by looking first for someone or something to blame. They prefer to think another person caused their failure. They believe that conditions throw obstacles in their path. They are sure that someone is working against them. They know they could succeed if certain basic things could be changed—always causes which they can blame on someone else.

Now ask yourself a few questions honestly.

Who is holding you back from doing the things you want to do? Who is keeping you from success? What is standing in your way? Why haven't you been able to pick yourself up and start over again?

Take the questions one by one, give them careful consideration, and you will come up with these answers:

No one can really keep you from doing the things you want to do, if you want to badly enough. The only one who can keep you from reaching success is the one who can keep you from keeping on, or trying again, and that person is you. The only thing that can stand in your way for long is your own attitude, an acceptance of failure or discouragement. And if you haven't been able to pick yourself up and start over again, it is because you simply haven't done it.

You may have had some small failure, or even a large one, in life, but that doesn't matter at all. The important question is "What are you doing about it now?" You may have been disappointed in other persons, discouraged with the results of something you have done, disheartened because your progress is slow, or even overcome for the moment by a blow that was completely unexpected —an accident, an illness or a demand on your services and time.

It doesn't really matter what happened to cause you to lose sight of your goal. But it is tremendously important to consider what you are going to do about it.

Miracle power gives you all the ability you need, not only to visualize and attain success, but also to overcome failure and disappointment, and to replace it with even greater accomplishment and prosperity than you had in the first place.

Miracle power, when you let it have full expression in your life, literally works miracles in removing the mountains of your own discouraged attitude, and even the mountains that may appear insurmountable in the world around you.

A man who called for spiritual help after a nervous breakdown said, "When you're down, you're down!" Miracle power is that which picks you up. It picked him up, when he began to change his attitude. In order to be healed, he had to stop saying he was "down" and start thinking "up," depending on the miracle power within him to take him there. Miracle power will lift you, too, out of whatever situation gets you down. Not only will it lift you, but it will take you higher than you have ever climbed before, when you learn to work with it and use it to a greater and greater degree in your life.

Why Did This Happen?

Individuals who are faced with problems usually ask, "Why did this happen to me?"

They ask "Why" with complaint in their voices, feeling that they have done nothing to deserve such a problem. They ask "Why" with a real desire to know what they have done wrong, so that they can avoid such mistakes in the future. They ask "Why," and they wonder.

Undoubtedly there have been, or are, times in your life when you ask, "Why? Why did this happen to me?"

There are always reasons for the things that come into human experience, and they are good reasons, based on the working of universal laws. But the reasons are not always easily uncovered.

If you can easily distinguish the mistakes you have made and correct them, you have profited by asking "Why," and this is good. But if you do not easily discover the answer, stop asking "Why," start awakening miracle power to clear away the debris of unfortunate experiences, and start building afresh.

Maybe you can see no reason why a particular situation should have come into your life, why a certain illness interfered with your plans, why you lost a job or a loved one, why you missed out on a promotion or a sale. But the reason isn't important. What does matter is where you go from here.

A new job can, and will, be better when you work with miracle power. Losing one friend may have prepared the way for a deeper, more lasting friendship. Missing out on a particular promotion can leave you free to take advantage of other openings. Work with miracle power, and you will discover how the greatest opportunities frequently come in the guise of difficulties or challenges. Drill for the oil in the situation, and you may come up with a gusher!

Miracle power can replace, repair or renew. It can build and bolster. It can bury the old disappointments, so that you will have room for the new hopes and aspirations. And, best of all, it can, and will, flow in to help you in your overcoming, and also in your new attainment. Miracle power is unlimited, and nothing is impossible to it!

"All Things Are Possible"

Remember this invincibility of the miracle power next time you are faced with a challenge. It is easy, in a human way, to think that nothing can be done, that there is no way out. But this denies the reality of miracles, and you must believe in miracles, brought about by the working of higher laws, if you are to open the valve and let the power flow.

Nothing is impossible. "With God all things are possible." (Mark 10:27 KJV) With the right use of miracle power in your life, you can remove the darkest clouds, paint the brightest sunrise and realize your greatest dreams and aspirations. You can, when you are willing to work with the laws that apply.

To remove mountains, to meet challenges, to overcome past errors, to strike oil even in unexpected places, apply the principle of faith, which is this:

Whatever you believe with all your strongest, deepest feelings, becomes true for you.

This is a universal principle that is now working in your life, whether you understand it or not, whether you believe it or not, whether you consciously cooperate with it or carelessly disregard it.

Many situations and conditions continue to remain in your life simply because you believe in them. You may even have been feeding them, nourishing them with your thoughts of problems and difficulties.

Now you can change the direction of your faith, and change the direction of your life.

Faith and feeling go together. So, whatever you feel deeply and believe strongly, is that which will be brought forth, or continued, in your life.

The human reaction to disappointment, failure, misfortune or a challenge of any sort is strong feeling. You, in a sense, pick up the thing that disturbs you and hug it tightly, literally fastening it to you with strong emotional ties. Before long it belongs to you. You have claimed it, and you continue to have it as a part of your life experience. You will keep on having the problem as long as you have strong feelings about it.

Challenges Are Opportunities

But try thinking about it this way. Every challenge, every situation that challenges you to your greatest effort, is an opportunity. And you can finish each problem experience with more than you had in the first place. You can, when you approach the whole situation with the idea of using miracle power, making the law work in your favor. Think of it as drilling for oil knowing that you are sure of finding it, because it is true that, rightly approached, every challenge that comes will yield its own reward to the victor.

Here is a formula for applying the principle of faith to every challenge that comes. It is also the formula for striking oil in these unexpected places.

It will help you make a new beginning, even when you have thought your life was over. It will take you from countless past failures into future success. It will change your mind, your surroundings, your life, your friends. It will make miracles happen, miracles that wipe out whatever is wrong and uncover new riches in the process.

The law of faith is this:

Whatever you believe with all your strongest, deepest feelings becomes true for you.

The formula is this:

Choose the idea of victory that best fits your particular situation, build a strong, feeling faith around it, and you can be victorious.

Suppose the challenge involves a failure of some sort: you had high hopes for a certain undertaking, but it didn't work out.

You could wrap yourself in a pall of gloom and settle back into the rut of not expecting anything better in life, or you can accept the situation as one of those unexpected places where an oil well is waiting to be discovered.

Understand for yourself that, when a plan falls through, it can only mean that there is something better for you. Fill your mind with the picture of something better, something more suitable and more richly rewarding that is coming to replace the past error.

Choose a new plan of victory, a new plan of attack, and back it up with all your strongest feelings. Make yourself become interested in the project of working out a new plan, visualizing new realms to be conquered. Build a strong, feeling faith in the spirit of success at work in your life, and then go forward in faith. Past failures will simply be forgotten as you strike oil by letting the miracle power work for you.

Interest Is a Key

One of the keys to making this formula work is the activating of your miracle power of interest.

You will never get very far on any project which doesn't really interest you, and this is true of any phase of life. Strangely enough, most people are much more adept at becoming interested in their problems than in their hopes and aspirations. They are content to go over and over the things that are wrong in their lives, but give only a passing thought to where they would like to go and what they want to accomplish.

Whatever the thing that goes wrong in your life, you can replace the problem with a rich blessing when you become interested in making this formula work.

Choose whatever idea of victory fits. It may be a picture of health to replace some lingering illness. It may involve happy relationships with other persons, to overcome feelings of inferiority and inadequacy. It might be a new business venture to replace the old one that didn't work out. But whatever your new aim is going to be, make sure it is one in which you can become interested, an idea that really appeals to you.

Let the miracle power help you seek out the idea of a new triumph which will fit into your scheme of things at this time. Then open all the channels, and let the miracle power of pure interest pour in to help you develop the picture.

Examine it from various angles; polish a little here, touch up a spot there. Be so interested that you begin to have a sense of identification with the new victory. Be so interested that you forget the problem or challenge that started it all. Jump into the new project with such enthusiasm and joy that you have to succeed. You can't miss!

Recognize that every challenge that comes carries within it a far greater blessing. Choose the idea of victory that best fits the situation, build strong faith feelings around it, and strike oil, even in the unexpected place. Do it, with interest and enthusiasm.

Fan the Fire of Enthusiasm

Enthusiasm, too, is a key to making this formula work. What starts as interest can be fanned into a fire of enthusiasm that literally carries you forward with its emotional impact. Build this enthusiasm, and you have found the source of oil. Enthusiasm, too, is a part of your miracle power.

Recently I ran across this capsule thought on a tea-bag tag line: "Convert the cold water thrown on your ideas into steam and forge ahead."

This provides a good analogy. We might compare the cold water to whatever serves to discourage you, the well-meaning comments of your friends or the failure of some plan in your life. But even this cold water itself can be turned into steam power to help you forge ahead into something better and greater than ever. And how is it done? By fire, which can be used here to represent the heat of enthusiasm.

Truly enthusiasm does enable you to ignore every reason why you might become discouraged and literally convert it into steam to provide the impetus you need to move into new and greater works.

With enthusiasm you are propelled forward so fast that many times you fail to even hear the pessimistic comments that others may make.

Without enthusiasm, all effort becomes a struggle, and very little is accomplished in the long run. But with enthusiasm, even the seemingly impossible becomes possible.

Feed the fire of enthusiasm as you work with new ideas, formulate new and greater plans for success, and then do the work that brings them forth.

It's easy to forget those disappointments of the past when you invest enthusiasm in new ideas, new plans and new projects.

Even those things which have never been done before can be done by one who not only has caught the vision, but also has the miracle power of enthusiasm working through him.

If you have wished to do something that seemed impossible, something that has brought only failure in the past, think of it this way: Enthusiasm is power, and when you have built up a head of steam, you also have propulsion power. With miracle power behind you, you can expect miracles to happen!

You can even build enthusiasm in the same way that you opened the channels for the power to come through in the first place.

Stride back and forth across the room, telling yourself "I am enthusiastic about life and living, and miracles happen to me!" Think in terms of the triumph you want to experience, and direct your enthusiasm toward that particular end. Build strong feelings around the idea; believe that you, working with miracle power, can do it, and then let the steam power built by your enthusiasm carry you forward into success.

Act the Part of Success

Build up your faith and enthusiasm about the new undertaking by acting the part you want to fill. You don't have to brag and strut about, trying to make an impression. But you can stop talking lack and start agreeing with the idea of abundance, in your mind and in your conversation. You can refuse to express any word of discouragement, but say always the optimistic, cheerful thing.

You can walk with head up and shoulders back, ready and willing to face the world and come out on top. You can take pains to dress yourself as a successful person would—not necessarily spending a lot of money on new clothes, but using care in donning the best you have, as you prepare the way for greater prosperity to come.

As a matter of fact, the worst thing you can do when faced by difficulties is to stay inside, wear old clothes, and revel in your difficulties. This attaches faith and emotion to the problem and makes it stronger than ever.

The next time you find yourself tempted to withdraw from the world and feel sorry for yourself, reverse the whole trend of your thinking by dressing up and getting out—if only to walk down the street with head held high, remembering that you are somebody after all.

Get back your perspective, re-establish goals and aims of good and build interest and enthusiasm in them. Let miracle power help you to get back on the right track through life.

You were not created to exist in a half-dead way for a certain number of years, but to live, to be alive, joyous and free, happy and successful. And any experience that comes to you in life can be handled in such a way that you are richer, happier and healthier when it is all over than you ever were before.

Even in the unexpected places, you can find clues to life and new impetus to help you carry through tremendous plans of good.

Miracle power won't work in spite of you, but it will work with you. And miracle power is unlimited!

Especially when you would find it easy to give in to discouragement or failure thoughts, turn on the miracle power in your mind. Use it to formulate new and greater plans. Use it to build interest and enthusiasm. Use it to strike oil—even where there seems to be no oil.

Whatever you believe with all your strongest, deepest feelings, becomes true for you.

Work with this law, and miracle power will bring you out of the doldrums and into the light.

Chapter 6

Live Happily with Yourself and Others

Miracle power can make you successful. It can make you healthy. It can bring you wealth, and will open avenues of wisdom beyond your present ability to imagine.

But perhaps the most important thing that miracle power can do is to make you happy.

Man's search for happiness is big business these days. Millions of dollars are spent in this country alone by people seeking to buy a few hours of enjoyment in one way or another.

"The Great Search" for Happiness

Many modern-day psychologists, having spent years of research to discover man's basic motivation in life, have come to the conclusion that man is motivated primarily by his desire for happiness. They refer to this striving for happiness as "the great search."

Perhaps you haven't considered a search for happiness your primary concern. But look at it this way: Inherent in every desire you have is the thought that you will experience an inward feeling of joy as the result of attaining that particular goal.

You want to be successful so that you will experience the joy of attainment. You want enough wealth to buy all the material things you feel will make you happy. You want to be wise, because there is an inner satisfaction in knowing. Even health will make you happier.

"The great search" usually takes you on a roundabout excursion. You follow first one rainbow and then another, expecting to find the treasure of happiness at the end. But somehow it doesn't work out that way.

You build all your hopes of happiness on one great attainment. And when you reach it, somehow there isn't the satisfaction you thought you would find. Instead, you discover another rainbow, promising yet another treasure at the end. But that, too, fails to make you completely happy. Again, you see something else beckoning.

You are always happy when you start out toward some goal that you feel will bring you satisfaction. There is a gladness in the search itself. But, when you reach the end, you experience a letdown feeling. You aren't happy as you thought you would be.

Why? Because it is the doing, the interest, that makes you happy. Reaching an end is nothing more than coming to a point where it is time to make a new beginning, to choose another goal and work toward it, again finding your greatest joy in the forward movement, being disappointed when it stops, and so on.

You can search for happiness in attainment. You can look for it in the acquiring of possessions. You can investigate the possibilities of happiness in recreation or hobbies. Most likely, you will at some time try to find happiness in relationships with other persons, through love, marriage, friendship or family life. And you will be disappointed in them if you fail to find happiness.

Strangely enough, every time you base your search for happiness on something outside of yourself, be it a person or a cruise to the South Seas, you will be disappointed—unless, of course, somewhere in your search you find the source of happiness where it lives, within yourself.

Happiness Happens through You

You will never find happiness in something outside yourself. It is only in your reaction to the outside stimulus that you discover that warm glow within yourself.

Nothing has any power to make you happy. Neither can anything make you unhappy. The same thing that makes one person happy may make another miserable. It depends on his reaction to it.

For instance, one of the happiest occasions at our home in the country is the time when we have a roaring fire in the fireplace on a cold, snowy evening, and enjoy the cozy atmosphere as we sit on the floor, roasting hot dogs and marshmallows over the fire.

This custom wouldn't appeal at all to many people. I know of one woman who refuses to have a fire in the fireplace because she doesn't want her curtains soiled by the smoke. Imagine her misery if she had to sit on the floor roasting hot dogs while mentally washing and ironing the curtains!

It's not the fire or even the companionship as we sit around the fire that makes this a happy time for us. It is the response of happiness that the whole atmosphere calls forth from within each one that makes it meaningful and enjoyable.

Your own happy times may be associated with entirely different situations—a breath-taking mountaintop view, a dip in the ocean, or an evening with old friends.

But look at those circumstances from another's viewpoint. I have known people from coastal areas who were so miserable in high places that they couldn't even look at a mountaintop view, and others who couldn't enjoy a dip in the ocean because of a fear of the water. Still others might not find your old friends entertaining at all.

So, you see, happiness is a very personal thing. It is the result of something that happens through you, not anything that happens to you.

Since this is the case, why not stop looking for happiness somewhere else, and let miracle power help you discover it where it is, within you?

The principle of happiness is this:

Look for happiness in other persons, places and situations, and you will never find it. But look for it within yourself, and you will discover it waiting there for you.

Then all you have to do is accept it.

You Are Designed for Gladness

A talent for happiness is already yours, whether you have developed it or not. Many talents lie dormant until they are awakened by your active interest, and the ability to be happy is one of the most frequently neglected.

It almost seems sometimes that people want to be miserable, that they are determined to reject every attempt to make them happy.

But you were created to be happy. And, if you are mentally refusing to accept the miracle power in you that wants to flow out as pure joy, you are making yourself even more miserable by this sublimation of your natural inclination.

You are supposed to be happy! You are created to enjoy every moment of life, to live fully and joyously all the time. You are designed for gladness and a sense of well-being.

Don't blame someone else if you aren't happy. Just go back and develop your God-given talent. Look for happiness where it is, within you, in a cheerful approach to life. And, if you find that you have forgotten how to enjoy life, then relearn the art of joy.

People are not naturally happy or naturally unhappy. They are what they are making themselves at any given moment. They are unhappy because they have decided to be unhappy, consciously or unconsciously agreeing with the idea. But they can become happy at any time simply by agreeing with that concept, the happy picture of themselves.

You can become happy at any time that you make up your mind to become acquainted with the source of joy within you, and you can't make the fullest use of miracle power until you have made this decision to enjoy life as well, because miracle power is joy power, and joy power is miracle power! Miracles happen to the one who has learned the art of being happy.

Gladness helps you to overcome fatigue. It heals even a broken heart. It attracts true popularity and success. It brings showers of abundance in whatever form is needed. It harmonizes, repairs, renews. It builds and bolsters. It has powers that haven't even been discovered yet, because it is one expression of miracle power.

Relearn the Art

If you have gotten out of the habit of enjoying life, and have learned to be miserable and unhappy, you may find that you have a job before you. But you have help as well. Miracle power will work for you when you open the way by searching for happiness where it is, within you.

It doesn't matter how long you have been unhappy. It doesn't matter how accustomed you are to being miserable. It doesn't matter at all how many things, people or situations you can find to blame for your troubles of mind and emotion.

You can be happy now, right where you are!

How do I know, when I don't even know the cause of your unhappiness? I know, because you were created to be happy. It doesn't matter what has come into your life to make you unhappy. It doesn't matter what other people have said or done, or how life seems to have treated you in general. You are designed to be happy, so start building gladness within.

Sometimes people have thought that a long face, a sober mien, was necessary to a religious or spiritual approach to life, and they have actually experienced a feeling of guilt when they were happy. But even this false idea can be vanquished.

Jesus Christ, the Man who is most quoted in religious circles today, said, "These things have I spoken unto you, that my joy might remain in you, and that your joy might be full." (John 15:11 KJV)

Joy is a part of the miracle power implanted in every man. It is there waiting to be claimed and experienced by you.

If you haven't been happy for some time, you may find the re-training of your feelings a hard task, but it is one that can be done, and miracle power will help you.

You didn't develop a habit of being unhappy in a moment, or even a day, and it may take time to break the habit of gloom. But it can be done.

Sell Yourself an Idea

First, sell yourself on the idea that happiness is not only your opportunity, but it is also your built-in talent and your right.

Talk to yourself in terms like this: "I am designed to be happy. I was created to find joy and fulfillment in life. I claim my right to happiness now."

Then do it. Don't wait for something to happen to you, but let joy happen through you. Don't sit around hoping someone will do something to make you happy, but just start feeling glad—about something, about anything. Learn all over again how it feels to be happy.

You may find it helpful to mentally review a time when you were happy. Close your eyes and relive the whole experience in your mind. Fill in details of green grass or the face of a loved one or a friend. Think how happy you were, and awaken that same feeling again.

Draw on your past experience to fill in the feeling of happiness.

Then open your eyes, and, remembering the way you felt on that happy occasion, declare, with feeling, that same feeling, "I can be happy now!" And be happy.

Don't base your happiness on the past experience, but use it only to remember how it feels to be happy, and then take that feeling with you. Find reasons for pleasure and enjoyment where you are.

Look around for something to appreciate. You should never let the possession or absence of things determine your happiness or unhappiness. But, just as an exercise in feeling the emotion of appreciation, choose some object that you especially value, and take a moment to be glad that you have it. Appreciation itself is a warm, happy emotion. Let it flow through your whole being, reminding you how it feels to enjoy something.

Refuse to let anything take this feeling away as you go through life, but continue to consciously agree with your right to be happy and your desire to develop this talent.

The more you give your attention to finding the source of joy within yourself, the more you develop your capacity for enjoyment of life. And the more you enjoy life, the more you experience wonderful activities of the miracle power.

So little is known of the principle of happiness that you may be surprised at some of the things that the miracle power of joy will trigger in your life. But, again, accept them with joy, and just keep on being happy.

Don't be afraid to be happy. Some people have an old idea that they must pay for their hours of happiness with other hours of misery. But this is true only when they believe it. And their belief is what makes it true for them.

You were designed to experience joy, all the time. Remember this and experience it!

Serve "Happy Soup"—and Eat It, Too

Happiness was made for sharing, and a part of your responsibility to the miracle power that brings it to you is passing it on to others.

The principle of sharing is this:

You can never give happiness away. The more you give, the more you have.

One day, in a supermarket I heard a young mother say to her little girl, "Oh, here's the happy soup. You remember I told you that happy soup is made by happy people. That's why it tastes so good when you eat it."

There is a good lesson in this snatch of conversation overheard in a grocery store.

Everybody needs some "happy soup" occasionally, a dish planned and executed in love and designed to bring happiness to others.

"Happy soup" can take the form of food prepared by a happy person and served in harmonious, happy surroundings. Surely this has the makings of a happy experience.

But "happy soup" can also take the form of nourishment for the soul, and perhaps that is the most important food of all.

Serve "happy soup" to your friends and loved ones in the form of a sincere compliment, a generous smile, and a happy laugh. Remember: ". . . happy soup is made by happy people." So the happier you are first, the more happiness you can give to others.

The compliment should not be forced, and neither should the smile or laugh. Let it be brought forth easily from within you, where the happy person is at work, the happy person that is the real you.

You can't make anyone happy or unhappy, any more than another person can force either extreme of emotion on you. But you can communicate a feeling of joy that speaks to the spirit of joy in him. And, if he is willing, he will feel the response of happiness from inside himself. Your own miracle power goes forth to awaken the spirit of happiness in others, and the miracle power of joy can work wonders, for them and for you.

Of course, the more experience you gain as one of the happy people manufacturing and distributing happiness, the happier you become in the process, because joy is something that you simply can't give away. The more you make and the more you give to others, the more you will have, and the more you will develop your capacity for being one of the happy people. That's the way it works.

Dissolve Inharmony with a Compliment

It is easy to manufacture happy soup and serve it to those who respond easily and like to share happiness with you. But happy soup, made by happy people, can even be served to those who have seemingly hurt you. It can be the means for dissolving a situation which has brought you disappointment and unhappiness in the past.

A friend enrolled in an adult evening class in sewing. She could sew a little, but thought she would like to improve her ability. She entered the class with a feeling of happy expectation, but after two or three classes was so discouraged that she decided she would either have to find some way to change the situation or withdraw from the class. The teacher, for no reason she could discover, seemed to have taken a dislike to her. She made pointed remarks designed to ridicule my friend and discourage her. It became so apparent that others in the class began to comment on it.

The student prayed about it and came up with this answer: "Maybe she doesn't feel secure as a teacher. Perhaps she is on the defensive because she thinks I know more about it than she does."

She determined to try one more time. The next class gave her an opportunity to try out her theory. When the teacher pointedly insulted her in the course of the lesson, she put all the enthusiasm she could muster into a sincere compliment as she said, "You are a wonderful teacher!" She really did feel that the teacher was doing a good job of instructing the class, and she put all of her conviction into the words. From that time on, all hostility vanished, and she thoroughly enjoyed the rest of the course.

You never know how much another person needs your gift of "happy soup" until you give it, and, when you do, you can never lose anything by it. Many times it comes back with interest.

Be the one who smiles first. Smile from the spirit of joy within you, and let the return take care of itself. Sometimes the person who has the most forbidding, frowning expression on his face is the one who is most in need of your smile. If you are going to live happily with yourself, you must also live happily with others—and do it first!

Smile for Your Sake

Consider the reasons why another may be frowning at the moment.

He may be concerned about pressing bills or worried about his job. He may be thinking, trying to plan some project in which he is involved, and may not intend to look unpleasant at all. He could be absorbed in hurry, mentally already coping with the next job in a busy schedule.

Serve him some happy soup in the form of a smile. Do it for your own sake, if not for his, because the more you share your own joy, the more you will have for yourself. The very act of giving a smile, a friendly greeting or a sincere compliment makes you feel good all over, and that is a sure sign that the miracle power of happiness is at work.

Sometimes the other person is just waiting for you to smile first. But if everybody stands around waiting for someone else to smile first, just think of the happiness-potential that is being wasted. But one smile may just set off a chain reaction, and the first one in the chain receives the greatest dividend. You can be the first to smile.

You are rich, when you have a smile to give. And you always have one waiting inside when you are working on the principle of happiness, when you are inviting the miracle power of joy to fill you so full of pleasant thoughts that they have to show in your face.

Be quiet sometimes, and just be happy. You don't even need a reason for happiness. Just feel joy. Let it well up and overflow. You are rich in joy right now. Feel it. Know it. Be it. Express it. And all the miracle power you can use will pour in to enrich your life and the lives of all the others you meet. It just works that way.

The principle of happiness is this:

If you look for happiness in other persons, places and situations, you will never find it. But look for it within yourself, and you will discover it already there, waiting for you.

And the principle of sharing completes "the great search" for you:

You can never give happiness away. The more you give, the more you have.

Work with these laws, and miracle power will teach you the rest. You can live happily with yourself and others, all the time.

Chapter 7

Overcome the Hurry Habit

Habits can be broken! And miracle power will help you do it.

Many people in our modern-day society have formed a habit which almost seems a way of life. They feel that it is necessary to conform to this habit, or they will be left behind.

These people rush from one thing to another, driving themselves, tense with hurry, fearing there will not be enough time to do the things that need to be done by them. They adopt haste and anxiety as a way of life, and then wonder why something unexpected comes to slow them down—an accident, a physical illness, or some other calamity.

They work from fear, and they push from pressure. If they continue to build up strain, tension, rush, push and anxiety, something has to give! Power must have a clear channel through which to express itself. It cannot flow freely when it is short-circuited by pressure on the line. If you refuse to slow yourself down, something happens to slow you down. How much better it is to slow yourself down, at your own convenience!

How much better it is to learn to turn on the current of miracle power and let it flow freely! How much more satisfactory it is to have continuous generation of energy to fill your needs!

Maybe even without realizing it, you have allowed pressure to build up. But when you recognize it, and its detrimental effect, you can do something about it.

Accomplish More in Less Time

You do not have to be put under pressure by the demands of today's society. You can be free to do everything in a divinely ordered way. You can let miracle power supply the steam, as you supply the outlets, when you work not from haste but from harmony and order.

When you learn to apply miracle principles for healing the hurry habit, you will discover that you can accomplish more in less time, with less strain, than you ever did in your life.

Strangely enough, the very tendency to hurry slows you down. It has to, because it shuts off the miracle power. Hurry is tension and strain, and stress literally closes off the power. That is why you become tired, irritable, anxious and nervous after having rushed all day. Instead of using the spiritual energy which is available to you, you are trying to do something yourself, and to force it at that! Hurry always implies force and pressure.

When you try to go through life in this way, hurrying, forcing, pushing, you use up all the strength and vitality that you do have, and do not leave the way open for more to flow in. You just keep spending until there isn't any more strength to spend, and you are forced to stop for a while.

It is well worth while to overcome the hurry habit, and to do it now, before it wastes any more of your God-given power and ability to accomplish.

Hurry and ease are direct opposites, but, strangely enough, ease is the one that gets the most done. It accomplishes more, because it leaves the way open for miracle power to work. It does a better job more quickly, because it facilitates the flow of mental and physical energy to do what needs to be done.

One who hurries has to become tense, because this is the nature of haste. Tension closes. Relaxation opens. This, then, is the principle of relaxation, as it applies to healing the hurry habit:

Relaxation opens the way for natural order to be established. Ease and order are the keys to accomplishment.

When you once begin to work with this principle, you will discover that you have more time than you ever had before. You may not be able to explain just how it works, but you will see that it does work. You can do more in less time by working with ease and relaxation. A miracle? Perhaps.

Relax before You Start

Of course, the best time to establish the relaxed attitude that leads to ease of accomplishment is in the beginning. Before you start out, you can set the mood for your day by establishing a relaxed attitude of mind and body. Before you start work on a new job, you can prepare for it by relaxation.

First of all, decide for yourself that you can relax. Many people have built up such a tremendous amount of pressure over a long period of time that they literally push themselves through life. If you laughingly say to them, "Relax! Take it easy," they seriously reply, "I can't relax." And they mean it. They honestly believe that they can't relax, and so their nerves and muscles respond to the command of their faith and continue to keep tension at a high pitch until something has to give and forces them to stop for a while.

If you have thought that you couldn't relax, or couldn't take time to stop and establish order, have a serious talk with yourself and establish a new understanding in your mind.

If you are going to live happily and successfully, if you are going to give your own supply of miracle power a channel through which to flow, you must learn to relax. And what you must do, you can do—not by trying to force the issue but by deciding to agree with what has to be done.

You can relax. You can immediately dissolve all tension, strain, anxiety, and fear at any time in any place. You can, if you are willing to believe that you can, or even to try believing long enough to give the miracle power a chance to help you.

It may seem hard to get started the first time you attempt it, but you will discover that the more often you practice relaxation, the easier it becomes, until it is almost second nature to let go when you notice the first signs of tension or hurry building up in your mind or body.

Establish a Pattern

To establish a pattern for relaxation, take time each day to learn the art of relaxing. Morning is a good time for this practice, because it prepares your mind and body for the business of living that day, in a sense of ease and order. And evening also provides a good occasion for relaxation. Always make it a point to relax before going to sleep, so that miracle power will have clear channels through which to flow for physical renewal while you rest.

For your specified time of releasing all tension, choose a chair in which you can sit comfortably upright. Put your feet flat on the floor and let your hands lie comfortably open in your lap. Then give your attention to the business of relaxation.

Sit quietly, close your eyes and take conscious control of your thinking. If you hurry in your mind and become anxious about the things that are waiting to be done, you can't give yourself to the practice of relaxing. So mentally push all pressing matters to the side while you concentrate on what you are doing.

As you sit quietly, think of letting go, letting go of problems, things waiting to be done, all pressures and anxieties—even happy things. With your hands open, mentally release everything that seeks to intrude, and give yourself over completely to re-establishing the natural order of your mind and body.

Then relax and let go. Mentally pass along this order to the nerves and muscles of your body, and expect them to obey. Feel them release all tension as you speak.

Speak to the nerves and muscles of your forehead. Tell them to relax and let go, and expect them to obey. Brush away all the hurry. A wrinkled forehead indicates tension. Just feel yourself mentally smoothing out the wrinkles, relaxing away from all sense of strain.

Go through all of your body, speaking silent words of release, relaxation, letting go. And then wait a moment for the response of release, before going on to the next. Speak to your eyes, your throat, the back of your neck. Work your way all the way down to your feet.

Revel in the feeling of completely letting go. Just feel good, as you give yourself up to the re-establishing of natural order in your mind and body.

Feel the new surge of strength and energy in every cell and atom of your being as you open the way for miracle power to flow in to renew and revitalize your whole body. Give yourself up to it. Relax in it.

Then, when you have completely freed yourself from all tension, get up and go about the business of the day. Carry the sense of ease with you. Don't try to make up for the time you have used in reaching this sense of relaxation. Rather, keep the awareness of natural order as you do the things that need to be done by you.

Do them one at a time. Don't anticipate future jobs and other matters awaiting your attention. Concentrate on the business at hand. Finish it, and go on to the next. You'll be surprised at the amount of work you can accomplish in one day when you work with the natural order of the universe, when you leave all the avenues open for miracle power to work through you.

You will do more, and you will do it without the strain and fatigue you have experienced after a day of rushing.

Avoid Costly Mistakes

Something else happens when you work from a sense of relaxation rather than from pressure. You don't make as many mistakes. It almost seems that the harder you hurry, the more you experience difficulties and setbacks. Things have a way of going wrong when they are forced. Materials break. Traffic jams develop. When you are hurrying the most, it seems that everything conspires to keep you from getting to your destination or finishing the task at hand.

Relaxation has the opposite effect. Even when it seems you must be late, a relaxed attitude will get you there on time. Even when you can see no way to accomplish what needs to be done, miracle power will show you how to do it, and do it through you, easily.

If you find that things start going wrong, and you have forgotten your earlier attitude of relaxation, you can return to it. Do it in your mind. Do it even when you are trying to make a deadline.

It might seem strange to make it a point to stop when you are hurrying to get somewhere or finish a job. But this is the very best thing that you can do. There is an old saying: "Haste makes waste," and if you keep forcing, you will only make for more waste.

Psychologists have proved, through time and motion studies, that you can accomplish more when you stop and rest at given intervals. If you continue to work without letup, rushing to finish something, you will take more time in the long run.

When you have re-established order in your mind, when the miracle power is again flowing freely through your body, then you are ready to resume your schedule. This time do it all in an orderly way, without tension or strain.

Relax and Think

Relaxation makes it easier for you to think clearly.

Stop and consider the way you feel when you are rushing to an appointment. Your mind literally becomes a jumble of half-explored thoughts as you let the tension mount. If you let it get completely out of hand, you will discover that you simply can't think clearly about anything. But this doesn't have to happen.

Relax, and think. Or we might put it this way: Relax, in order to think. Let go of your tense, anxious search for an answer, and let miracle power flow in to think through you.

Use the following method to get rid of hurry in your thinking and to re-establish order in your mind:

Whenever you find yourself rushed or anxious, disturbed or confused, stop and clear your mind of all tension.

Release the thought of the answer you seek, and let your mind be at peace. Stop trying to apply logic or to force your thinking. Just relax and let the miracle power flow through your mind.

Silently speak to your mind and your thinking processes such words as "calm," "peace," "serenity." Let the ideas they convey take hold and establish a picture of serenity and peace. Stop trying to think anything specific. Just quietly let the peace flow through your mind and thoughts.

Your mind relaxes most effectively when your body is also relaxed.

So let your body be established in a comfortable position and then forget it while you let your thoughts be filled with calmness.

Then, when you are completely relaxed, mind and body, open yourself to the Source of ideas within you, the miracle power of your mind. Don't take any problem with you. Simply open your mind to the ideas you need.

A promise from the Bible tells of the miracle power in your mind. In the Book of Isaiah, it is written, ". . . before they call, I will answer; and while they are yet speaking, I will hear." (Isaiah 65:24 KJV)

The idea and the understanding that you need are already available to you. Before you even discover your need, the answer has been provided for you, lodged in the miracle potential of your mind.

Discover it for yourself. Relax your mind and body and open yourself to the answer you seek by saying, "I am relaxed and receptive. All that I need to know is revealed to me now."

Then let go and let the miracle power, or God idea, flow easily into your mind. Relax, and you will find it easy to think clearly.

Make a Friend of Time

Many people allow their lives to be ruled by time because they are afraid of it. They are afraid there will not be enough time to do all they need to do. They fear the passing of time, and dread other occasions when time may lie heavy on their hands.

There is a principle for learning to get along with time, and it is this:

Make a friend of time, and you will never have to hurry again. If you have ever had the hurry habit, you have been afraid, because fear is always the reason for hurry. You were afraid there wouldn't be enough time. You were afraid of being late.

But time is not your enemy; it is your friend. Recognize this, and you have made a friend for life, one that will help but never hinder. When time is your friend, in your mind, then every moment is filled with miracles, and there is no room for fear. There is a momentary, complete, joyous acceptance of the good in your life.

Your life is not measured by time, as such, but by the use you make of it. After seventy, eighty or ninety years measured by days and hours and minutes, your life will not be calibrated by the length of time you have lived, but by the use you have made of that time.

One year, one month, one hour, even a moment can be made to count tremendously. The span of time is only important when it is filled with happy, productive activity. The same period devoted to self-indulgence, laziness or boredom is nothing but a waste of a precious commodity.

Each hour of your life will be just what you make it. It will bring you joy and accomplishment or hurry and confusion, love and peace or fear and failure. The secret of making time work for you lies in making it your friend, one that serves you in a divinely ordered way as you go about the business of living according to your best understanding at the present time.

Welcome the Moment

Welcome each moment as it comes to you. Invite it in to share your joy, and you will be surprised at how many moments there are, and what happiness they can bring into your experience. Welcome time as it arrives, give it your best hospitality and service, and it will always serve you well, without fuss, without strain, and with benefits beyond anything you expected.

Other friends may come and go in your daily experience, but time is one friend you have always with you. It can be a good companion when you establish a relaxed, harmonious relationship with it.

Time will always be to you what you make it. If you treat it as an enemy, it almost seems to fight back, because no matter how hard you try to hurry, you will always be late, and no matter how hard you work, you will never finish what needs to be done by you.

Many people speak of "working against" time to get something done. This is exactly what they do. They build up pressure and anxiety and, in a sense, fight time all the way. How much better it is to welcome time and let it work for you instead!

If you start resisting time, it seems that it resists you right back, but this isn't really what happens. The resistance is all in you, in your mind. Time is neutral. It is waiting for you to name it, to determine its nature and its expression in your life. You do this by your attitude, either treating it as a friend or fighting it as an enemy. Time itself doesn't change. It just lets itself be used by you in the manner which you determine for yourself.

Of course, once you have made friends with time, you may on occasion treat it like a member of the family, even forgetting about it entirely as you go easily about the business of living. It fits into the pattern you make for it.

Every moment of every day holds many opportunities for joyous, productive living. If you are not wasting your power in fighting time, you will be wide awake and ready to discover the good that time offers as you pass through life.

In a sense, time itself is a miracle. No one can explain exactly how or why it comes, what it is all about. But it is here, another gift of the Creator, waiting to be named by you, seeking to serve you in whatever way you determine for yourself. It is a free gift, without strings attached. The only strings that can be tied to it are those you tie yourself.

You determine what time will mean to you, whether it will be an enemy you fight, a boring acquaintance that you can't escape, or a friend you welcome into your home.

Hold time with open hands; don't try to clutch it. Welcome the moment as it comes, and then bless it on its way. Anticipate happy experiences in the future, but don't let anticipation blot out today. Seek out the joy and the love, the peace and the plenty here, now, where you are, in this present moment. Live it fully. But live it easily, without haste. Savor it as you would a well-prepared meal, and then go on to your next moment in living.

Time is too important to be wasted in hurry. It is too valuable to be killed in boredom. Learn to treat it kindly, and it will serve you well!

Miracle power will help you heal the hurry habit. It flows in easily to harmonize and establish order when you begin to work with the principle of time:

Make a friend of time, and you will never have to hurry again.

Chapter 8

Flow with the Current of Health

You were designed for health, and miracle power will help you express it!

It doesn't matter what has happened to your physical body in the past. If you have a sincere, deep-down desire to establish vigor and vitality, order and strength in your body, and if you are willing to back it up with understanding and action, you can awaken the miracle power that will not only heal, but also establish health in your mind, body and affairs.

Health is your natural state. You were designed to express complete well-being, all the time and in every way. Your body is a self-repairing, self-renewing mechanism. It is engineered to operate perfectly. You are supposed to be healthy. You have been put here on this earth to accomplish great things, and you have been given all the equipment you need to carry the project through to a successful conclusion. The equipment includes the potential of a perfect body.

This is a body that is not supposed to wear out in a certain number of years, but is constantly renewing itself, so that the atoms you are using today are completely different from those which made up your physical being five years ago.

The body through which you are now expressing yourself can be healed if there is anything wrong! It can be strengthened, vitalized, renewed. It can be transformed by the action of miracle power. Even if you are already healthy, it can be made healthier, stronger, more vital and alive. Your body is designed to serve you perfectly in the business of living, and it will do it, when you are willing to awaken, and to work with, the miracle power within you.

Are You Ready for Healing?

First, you must decide that you want to be healed, strengthened, harmonized and vitalized.

Many people who think they would like to be healthier are not really ready for health. Deep down within themselves, they may even have a fear of healing. With wholeness will come responsibilities. Are they ready for them? Do they want them?

Examine your own thinking closely, and see whether you want the miracle power to become active in your body. If you are absolutely strong and healthy, you may be deprived of some very comfortable excuses for not doing the things you would rather not do. You will have certain responsibilities to life. You will be responsible, too, to the miracle power which heals. You will be liable for using rightly the strength and power that flow in to bless your body, and yourself. You cannot sit back and watch the drama of life unfold. You will have to get up and participate in the action. Are you ready for this?

You may have to take a job, if you haven't been working. You may have to do other things.

Consider another factor in healing. If you are well, you will no longer have the pleasure of telling others about your aches and pains. (If you do, you will just re-create them in your body, as well as in your mind.) You cannot demand, and receive, sympathy from others healthier or happier than you. You will have to enter into life without those crutches of conversation and human relations that you may have depended on for some time. Are you ready to throw away the crutches?

If you are, then learn the principles of health and healing, and get ready for health! Open the way for miracle power to flow through, and you will have physical strength and power beyond anything you have imagined!

Turn to the Built-In Intelligence

Earlier in the book we considered the principles of recognition and appreciation as they apply to health and healing. Now consider another principle of healing, and prepare for miracles. The principle is this:

Your body is a self-repairing mechanism. Open the way for its built-in intelligence to direct the action, and you will be healed.

This is the way it works:

Your body, without your interference, automatically and intelligently functions in a perfect way. It is designed to do so. Your breathing continues, whether you think about it or not. Your blood circulates, and all of the other physical functions proceed in an orderly manner, except when you interfere with the action.

Every tiny cell in your body is equipped with the intelligence to do its job perfectly. Don't blame the I.Q. of your body if it fails to function properly; each minute part of your physical mechanism not only knows how to perform its usual work in a perfect manner, but it even has the know-how to detect the slightest deviation when it occurs and to make whatever corrections are necessary. It can institute repairs and carry them through in perfect order. Left to itself, your body has no problems, because it is a self-renewing, self-repairing organization of intelligent parts.

But your body isn't left to itself. Its own innate knowledge is subject to a higher intelligence, that of your mind. Like a well-trained army, your body responds to the orders you give it, and if those orders are not in keeping with the perfect plan, you are in trouble!

You direct your body by means of thoughts, words, actions, reactions, emotions. Anything which affects you, affects your body. That is the way it works.

When you become upset or disturbed, your body becomes upset or disturbed. If you have an argument while you are eating, don't blame your stomach if it serves up a dose of indigestion. You give the orders, and your body jumps to obey.

Don't blame your body if it fails to function properly, but go back to the commanding officer and make sure he is giving the right orders. You are your own commanding officer. Make sure you are giving the right orders.

The built-in intelligence of every cell in your body is another expression of miracle power, but, again, it is a power which can work only when you turn the switch and let it flow.

Miracle power can heal. It can establish harmony and life. But it can work only under your direction and with your acquiescence. Your body is subject to your orders, and it will do what you give it to do.

Give it the order to operate according to its own built-in intelligence, and that's what it will do.

Your Body Gets in on the Act

There are many ways in which you do give orders without realizing that you are doing it.

For instance, suppose you become angry. You lose your temper, and you say things you may later regret. That is a part of the effect, but it is only a part. Anything which affects you, affects your body. You can't become emotionally disturbed without having a physical reaction as well. When you are angry, your heart races, your breathing is disturbed, your muscles tighten; these are just a few of the reactions. If you lose your temper often enough, you can work up a pretty good case of apoplexy or high blood pressure. Something is bound to happen in your body if you keep giving it orders to become upset.

You also instruct your body with the words you speak. It works this way:

Suppose you say "So-and-So makes me sick!" and then go on to detail all the things in another person that disturb you mentally and emotionally. If the other person is allowed to make you sick mentally and emotionally, you can be sure that your body will get in on the act, too. Pretty soon it will begin to respond to your orders to be sick.

The cells of your body are intelligent, but they can't differentiate between what you mean and what you don't. When you speak of being sick, like the good soldiers they are they jump to obey your command. You body is sick, too. It could just as easily be well, but when you tell it to be sick, it responds to your instruction.

Perhaps you unthinkingly have allowed certain things to "eat on" you, a worry, a resentment, or some unpleasant memory. You may even have said, "The memory of that just keeps eating on me!" If it gnaws at you mentally and emotionally, pretty soon it will eat on your body, too. How often the worries of modern life "eat on" the individual until he develops a case of ulcers!

Remember, your body takes what you say literally and works diligently to bring about the condition you decree. It will work even more diligently to restore health, when you begin to activate miracle power by giving the right commands.

Words and expressions, even carelessly or thoughtlessly spoken, may serve to intensify certain concepts in your mind until your body moves to make them so in fact. It just follows orders.

Perhaps you have been using slang expressions thoughtlessly, or throwing out negative suggestions in your conversation. If you are having physical problems, this may be the root of your trouble. Remember, your body can't take a joke. It considers whatever you say an order from headquarters and does its very best to obey your command. You must learn to give it the commands you want to see obeyed, if you are going to be strong, healthy, alert and alive.

The natural tendency of your intelligent body is toward health. So when you consciously direct it in that way, it co-operates even more willingly in establishing the right ideas.

Automatic Repairs

Your body knows how to repair itself. All you have to do is to give it the green light to go ahead and do it.

Even without your conscious co-operation, it automatically makes many repairs—unless, of course, you interfere.

Suppose you cut your finger. Many times, if it seems a minor injury, you wash it and forget it. The healing goes on automatically. All of the cells that are involved in forming a protecting scab, healing, knitting and replacing go about their business in an orderly manner and come up with a healing job so complete that in many cases you can't even tell that the finger was injured in the first place.

You might call it a miracle, if you weren't so accustomed to this sort of thing.

But what happens when the injury seems to be more serious? Do you still trust the intelligence of your body to make repairs? It can, but it can only work on your orders. If you ask for healing, but think worry and concern, the body responds to whatever orders you speak most loudly in your mind and in your emotions.

Sometimes the act of having medical help will increase your faith so that you can activate the miracle power to heal. Doctors treat, and nature, or God, heals. But it is your attitude that determines what help you will have. The treatment is only as effective as your body's acceptance of it. And miracle power can only flow through the channel that is opened to it.

Most physicians now say that cheerful, optimistic patients experience a quicker, surer healing than those who are depressed and negative in their outlook. Of course they do, because they are flowing with the current of life, they are activating their own built-in repair system, and they are in tune with the medical help they are receiving. They have everything working for them! On the other hand, one who is depressed in mind is depressing the intelligent cells of his body, and they simply can't get up and do the healing work.

If you believe that you can be well, and can see yourself, in mind, strong and healthy, you are on your way to healing. Put the miracle power to work by your complete acceptance of it, and you will be well!

Physicians generally agree that they would much rather operate on a person who expects to recover than on one who believes he is going to die, regardless of what the trouble may be. Such is the power of the mind in healing. And miracle power is even greater!

The Current Carries You Along

To a greater or lesser degree, miracle power is working all the time, almost in spite of the obstacles you place in its way.

Many healings take place automatically. You never even become aware that something is wrong. The constant renewing, restoring activity of your body intelligence continues on its way, except when you interfere with its activity by your mental or emotional orders to it.

In a sense, the miracle healing power is a current that is constantly flowing through you, trying to carry you back to the perfect idea you were designed to express. It is flowing all the time, and it carries you with it when you are willing to go along. You can choose to go along all the time and let the built-in intelligence of every cell take care of all your needs for bodily healing. You can learn to co-operate completely with the current as it flows to the sea of perfection.

You may build a dam and stop the stream of health for a time, but once you break through your own barriers and re-establish the free flow of miracle power, the healing current gets back into its channel, and miracles of healing follow. The Intelligence that created your body in the first place implanted within it all the knowledge needed to restore it at any time. Your job is to prepare the way for the built-in intelligence to work. When you do, you will be healed by the orderly action of the power in you.

Feel Good All the Time!

The current of miracle power will also enable you to express perfect health as a normal state of being. It is designed to maintain the well-being of your body, as well as to restore it when it is out of order. And once you learn to work in harmony with the current of health, you will find that even the sense of well-being you have experienced in the past is less than that which you will have through complete co-operation with miracle power.

You should feel good all the time. You were created to be healthy, happy, strong and alive all your life. Learning to ride the current of miracle power will heal your body, and will not only maintain health but also increase your strength, your vitality and your general sense of well-being.

This is the principle of health:

When you relax and swim with the current in yourself that knows the way of health, you will experience health and wholeness as a way of life.

The principle of relaxation applies in moving with the current of health. You simply can't go with the current unless you are willing to trust it, and relaxation is a part of trust. Tension is the enemy of the swimmer, and it is the enemy of health as well.

One who becomes tense and anxious while trying to swim never gets very far very fast, and, before it is all over, he may find himself sinking and calling for help.

The same idea applies in riding the current of health. You have to learn to relax in order to become a good swimmer in the current in yourself that knows the way of health. And relaxation is a part of the process.

Relaxation opens the way for natural order to be established in mind, in body, and in affairs. Physical relaxation and a relaxed attitude of mind are necessary to the expression of perfect health.

Relaxation does not mean doing nothing. Rather, it means releasing all tension so that normal activity can continue.

Your body's built-in guidance system is completely programed with the knowledge it needs. It can strengthen and vitalize as well as repair, and it will, when it is allowed to conduct the operation of your physical being.

Relax; trust in the intelligent current in you that knows the way of health, and you will open the way for miracle power that is greater than anything you could have experienced in your human understanding.

Flowing with the current of health doesn't mean just doing nothing. It means, rather, actively co-operating with it. When you flow, you don't just float. You move easily with the current of life, correcting your course when it seems in order but trusting the water of life to hold you up, not fighting, but moving with the miracle power, letting it do its work as you welcome it, co-operate with it, and relax into it.

Try it sometime. With complete trust in the miracle power, relax and co-operate with the Intelligence that heals and vitalizes your body from within.

"In God We Trust"

You can awaken an even greater power for healing and for health by applying these principles on the spiritual level of understanding. This is illustrated by the story of a little girl who was to have a minor operation.

The child was unable to take an anesthetic, and the doctor decided to let her use her power of concentration instead.

Before the operation he put a half dollar in her hand and said, "This is for you to spend as you like. But now I want you to take a good look at it, then hold it tightly and think of what you saw."

When the operation was over, he asked what she thought about while he was working. She replied, "The words!"

The little girl went on to explain, "It was the first half dollar I ever saw, and I didn't know the words were there. But I think it's lovely. People who have half dollars can think about them all the time."

The words were "In God We Trust."

The doctor was employing a basic principle when he gave the child the coin to study before the operation. When her attention was centered on something of interest, the element of pain would be less disturbing. But how wise the little girl was to pick the words of reassurance from the face of the half dollar!

Miracle power is God-power. Nature at work is God at work. The very intelligence that is implanted in your body and does the healing work through you is God-intelligence.

You can have wonderful results of healing and health simply by working with these principles. But if you want an even stronger current of the healing life activity, call the miracle power God-power. Put your trust in God. Relax into His goodness. Believe in His activity of life and health and strength and general well-being in you. Believe in it, identify with it in your mind, co-operate with it in your feelings, and put your trust in God.

Call on any physical or medical help you need in time of difficulties, but know that health and healing are both the result of the divine spark implanted within you. The things that are impossible with man in his human understanding are possible with God.

Health is your divine right. It is one of your many gifts from God.

But God's gifts must be accepted. Recognize the Source. Understand that the current in you that knows the way is just a little bit of God in expression. Accept the gift of wholeness by learning to relax into God's current in you, and to swim with it.

Be cheerful and optimistic. Refuse to discuss physical problems with friends. Relax and swim in the current of health and healing. Trust in God. And all the intelligent forces of your body will speed to establish God's perfect work in you.

Chapter 9

Get Rich by Miracle Methods

Miracle methods will make you rich!

Basic laws are always in operation to establish your prosperity, or lack of it. Conscious co-operation with these principles can bring you true and lasting riches of mind, body and affairs. Miracles happen when you learn to recognize, and work with, the universal laws of supply.

As you do, don't limit yourself! You will be surprised at the abundance that can come to you when you obey the universal laws and leave the way open for miracle power to provide all you can use, good measure, pressed down, and shaken together, and running over.

Goodness Versus Prosperity

First, understand that goodness and abundant supply go hand in hand for the one who works with miracle power.

If you have had some idea that you had to be poor to be good, get rid of it now, before you go any further. You will never have all the riches you are supposed to have if you have any feeling of hesitancy and guilt about acquiring wealth.

Understand that riches of mind and affairs are not given to you to be hoarded, but to be used. And the more you have, the more good you can do in your world. You are supposed to have just as much as you can use wisely and well. You are not to acquire so much that it will become a burden to you.

Seen in this light, riches are an asset, not a liability. They represent a part of the universal plan of good for all men. And your riches are given to you for the purpose of enriching others as well. On the other hand, your refusal to live in the miracle world of abundance deprives others of good, as well as you.

Probably the idea that one must be poor to be good was started by someone who was living in lack, one who made up for his own feeling of inadequacy by parading his lack as goodness.

Many people do wear lack as a badge of goodness. They parade it in front of their friends and even seek to arouse a sense of guilt in those who have more of material wealth. They tell the world in their own particular manner that they must be especially good, because they are so poor! And they may sincerely believe it.

This is not necessarily true. A man may be good, in many ways, and live in lack because he doesn't understand the laws of prosperity. But the fact that he is poor is no gauge of his goodness. It simply means that he hasn't applied the principles of supply.

Abundance is a part of the divine plan for the universe. It is in keeping with all of the expressions of nature, with its prolific production of everything from leaves on the trees in the summertime to snowflakes in the winter.

And it is easier to work on a plane of high ideals and the right use of your God-given abilities when you are well fed and unworried about affairs of finance.

The Camel and the Needle's Eye

Sometimes the idea of goodness and lack is tied in with a religious connotation. Someone may quote these words of Jesus Christ: ". . . It is easier for a camel to go through the eye of a needle than for a rich man to enter into the kingdom of God" (Matt. 19:24 KJV), inferring that the rich man and the kingdom of God have no common meeting ground.

But take another look at the wording of the instruction. The Master Teacher said: "It is easier for a camel to go through the eye of a needle," but he didn't say it was impossible for "a rich man to enter into the kingdom of God."

Many authorities believe that Jesus referred to a city gate in Jerusalem called the Needle's Eye. This was a small gate. It was impossible for a heavily loaded camel to pass through, but a camel without a load could pass through easily.

When Jesus referred to the rich man entering into the realm of the greater good, he didn't say it couldn't be done. He indicated the way in which it could be done. One who is possessed by his possessions will have to stay outside. But if he is willing to unload the camel, to get rid of the excess, then the unloaded camel can be passed through easily.

Great wealth carries with it an obligation: Under universal law, the more you have, the more you are responsible for using wisely. If you find that you are running into difficulties in entering new areas of growth, try lightening the load through giving. You will be surprised at how quickly and easily a release of the excess will open the way for other blessings to come to you.

Having material wealth does not make you good. Neither does living in poverty. In either case, it is a question of applying certain principles in your daily life.

If you really want to live in the flow of miracle power, you will work with the principles of prosperity in such a way that you always have everything you need, without being burdened by excess.

No matter how little or how much you have, it is your attitude that determines not only your essential goodness, but also your right relationship to the things that you do, or do not, possess.

The poor man can be possessed by envy of the things he doesn't have to such an extent that he is more obsessed by his lack than a rich man may be attached to his possessions. On the other hand, a rich man can learn to enrich others as well as himself and joyously fulfill his responsibility to his wealth. It is all in the attitude of the individual.

You are as rich, this moment, as you can think in your mind. You are as good, right now, as you are in your thoughts.

Fill your mind with ideas of abundance, seek a greater knowledge of, and identification with, goodness, and you will find that you can live happily and richly, too.

Poor Charlie!

I read a news story one time about a man named Charlie Cooper, who described himself as "the unhappiest man in Britain." The headline read "Poor Charlie."

Most people would like to be in Charlie's shoes, or they think they would. Practically everyone has, at some time, a dream of the sort of windfall Charlie had. But it didn't make Charlie happy.

He just won 225,000 pounds, about $630,000 in American money, in a British soccer pool at the time that he described himself as "the unhappiest man in Britain."

He explained, "If it had been 2000 pounds or 20,000 pounds, I would have been happy. But this is too much for a man like me—much too much."

This man had been working as a $29-a-week clerk, and, after he left his job and bought a new umbrella, he simply didn't know what to do with the rest of the money.

Wealth of any kind carries with it responsibilities, and money alone is never the answer to all a man's problems. Money is to be used, not hoarded. It is to be respected, but not worshiped. It is to be a joy, not a burden.

I never saw another story about Charlie, but I feel sure that unless he learned to cope with his wealth, he never really felt himself rich at all.

Most people are not given a great deal of money or many material possessions suddenly. And this is a good thing, because, unless one is ready for wealth, unless he has the confidence and know-how to handle it wisely, he will neither enjoy it nor use it as it should be used.

How much better it is to learn to co-operate with the universal principles of wealth and to grow into a greater ability to handle money and possessions. Then rich living is not a matter of suddenly acquiring a great deal or of hoarding that which has been given. It is, rather, living in the flow of the circulation of wealth through the universe, always having abundance, but never being burdened by it.

Wise is the one who learns to work with the principle of giving, which is this:

Universal law works constantly to maintain a balance in all things. Therefore, "Give, and it shall be given unto you; good measure, pressed down, and shaken together, and running over, . . ." (Luke 6:38 KJV)

And when you are working with the law of giving, while you will always have more supply returning to you, you will never be burdened, but will always live richly. That is the way it works when you let the miracle power flow freely as abundance in your life.

Give Because You Want to

Don't give grudgingly, because you have to. Don't give selfishly, because you want to receive. Do give richly, because you are a free and joyous channel through which miracle power flows freely. The return will always take care of itself.

Perhaps you have resented the efforts of others to force you to give. The raising of money for many different causes has become a high-pressure business. You may have been approached so frequently and so forcibly that the very thought of giving arouses antagonism within you. And yet you may feel that it is expedient to give to certain causes because of the human feelings that are involved in the situation.

Don't let yourself be forced into giving. If you don't give willingly, your contribution loses much of its value, for you and for the recipient. Instead, put your own personal reactions aside, go within yourself to your own powerhouse of mind and turn on the miracle power to give you your answer. Stop and listen to the voice within that tells you where, what and how much to give.

Then give—freely, cheerfully and with the joyous understanding that, as you give, you will receive even more richly as nature restores the balance.

One who comprehends the principle of giving wants to give, under the direction from within. One who does not understand will not find joy or satisfaction in a donation that is forced; neither will he benefit truly from the working of the law of giving and receiving.

Don't try to gauge your giving by the giving of others, but turn to the voice in you that knows your need to give at this particular time. Give joyously and willingly, and release the gift as you go on to your next experience in living. You may be surprised when your good comes back to you, good measure, pressed down, shaken together, and running over.

Give Yourself Out of Debt

You can use this same principle to give yourself out of debt, or out of a situation of lack.

The less you have, the more urgently you need to give something. It is only through giving that you can open the channels for greater abundance to flow in. Giving, in a sense, is an expression of faith in the universal law. And giving, no matter how great your need, is absolutely necessary to turn on the miracle power to bring prosperity into your life and affairs.

If you are in debt, don't sit around wishing for enough to pay all your debts, but start in to give what you can. If you can't pay the full amount, pay what you can. When you do what you can, with full trust in God or the working of universal law to do the rest, you'll be surprised at how quickly, easily and completely miracle power can work to solve your most urgent problem of lack.

And, before you pay, give something!

Tithing, the orderly, systematic giving of one tenth to God's work, is one way of opening the channels for abundance to come through. This is a good method, because it is based on the idea of giving first, with the full expectation that there will always be plenty to meet every need. This is a method that works.

I know a woman who had to give up her job to stay home and care for an elderly relative. Her income was so small that before long she found herself burdened by debts. She didn't know what to do or where to turn until she remembered my prosperity class she had attended one time.

When she remembered, she called and told me about her plight. Then she said, "I remember what you told us about tithing as a way to prosperity. I am going to start tithing to the church, and I know it will help me out of my difficulties."

She was systematic about it. Every Monday mail brought her check and a report of her situation. As the weeks passed, the checks grew larger, and the bills were gradually cleared up, until one day she wrote, "There is just one more debt, and I know that will be paid in a few days." She continued to tithe, and continued to prosper.

Tithing is one method of systematic giving that turns on a regular flow of miracle power, so that there is always plenty to meet every need, with some to spare.

Miracle power requires an open channel through which to flow, and giving is the best way to open it. Withholding, in fear of lack, will close it every time.

Accept Your Good!

Give, and then follow another universal principle, the principle of acceptance:

Supply has many ways of coming into your life. To take the greatest advantage of your opportunities, leave all the doors open, and actively work with the miracle power by accepting your good when it arrives.

Many people limit themselves by feeling that they must receive what they need in a certain way. But this is not true. There are many different, even unexpected, ways in which your particular good can come. You can look in one direction only and miss all of the other blessings that are passing by unnoticed, or you can leave all the channels open and live richly all the time.

Do you believe that you can have more money only by receiving a raise in pay? Do you feel that you must wait to pay your bills until a certain person repays you? Do you think that you shouldn't accept some gift from another person, for fear of depriving him?

Now stop and think about miracle power. Do you really believe that it can be confined to just one small channel? Can you look out on a starry night, try to count the many universes beyond ours, and believe in a limited supply?

Put yourself in tune with the universal plan, and you will see that all of life and living is designed for abundance, and good has many channels through which to flow.

There is only one limitation that applies, and that is the size of the aqueduct you construct to bring supply into your life. If you keep it small by saying, "I only have this much, and I can only hope for that much," you can be sure that miracle power itself can't break down the dam of the mental limitations you have set.

Others Need to Give, Too

A woman who is living on welfare payments has told me her troubles from time to time. Her conversation is sprinkled with such statements as this: "I only have so much a month. I can't expect to have any more, or my welfare will stop." "I ate lunch at the ten-cent store. I only had a sandwich and coleslaw, but I really couldn't afford that."

She does volunteer work, a form of giving which brings her return blessings from time to time. But she won't accept them. Even when a neighbor invited her to have a glass of milk, she said, "No, thank you, I have plenty at home," though she didn't. She simply refuses to accept the good that comes to her.

There is something else she does when she turns down the gifts of others: She deprives them of the privilege of giving!

The law of giving works for everyone. Don't just apply it for yourself and refuse the other person's gift when he seeks to give to you.

Perhaps you have had the idea that if you accept something from another person, you are depriving him of some material thing that he needs.

The principle of giving works for everyone. The one who has the least needs to give the most. He must give, if he is to open the channel for receiving more. Open the way for his greater supply by graciously accepting that which he offers.

Prosperity is not supposed to be the property of a few. It is most satisfactory and most effective when it is a group project. This means working with the idea of circulation, a balance of giving and receiving, the natural, orderly flow of good through the universe.

Circulation Is Life

Circulation is the key to the healthy economic life of individuals as well as of nations and whole economies. It is miracle power in action.

Nature works constantly to establish a balance, and nature works best in the atmosphere of free circulation. This is easily seen in the operation of the human body, but it is a principle which also works in the lifeblood of the economy of individuals and nations.

When something happens to cut off the free circulation of air through your lungs or of blood through your body, you experience physical difficulties. When you stop the circulation of wealth in your affairs, either by refusing to give or by refusing to receive, you cause an unhealthy condition.

Circulation is life. Stagnation is death. This is true in your physical body, and it is true in your prosperity.

Whole nations have experienced diseases caused by a stoppage in the flow of wealth. One such disease is commonly called a depression.

Depressions usually begin with "tight money." For some reason, people are afraid to spend their money, banks are afraid to lend, employers are afraid to hire more workers, and it all adds up to something that acts as a communicable disease. The more it is discussed, the worse it gets, until free circulation of wealth gives way to stagnation and debt, poverty and want—in other words, a depression.

You will find it easiest to prosper when others prosper as well. But even when others become fearful and try to cut off the circulation of wealth, you will always have all the material good you can use, when you keep a free circulation active in your affairs. Miracle power will help you to do it. And miracle power, working in and through the affairs of individuals, helps the nation as a whole.

The more people are applying the laws of giving and receiving, the better the state of the economy as a whole.

Miracle power must have channels through which to flow, avenues through which to express itself. But, once it is released, miracle power is unlimited!

Establish prosperity in your own affairs by giving freely and receiving graciously. Let wealth circulate in your life, and you will always have plenty. You will contribute, too, to the prosperity of others.

Miracle power is circulation, and circulation is life!

Chapter 10

Improve Personal Relationships

In order to be successful in today's way of life, you must learn to get along with other persons. And miracle power will help you do it!

Your job depends on happy human relationships. Your happiness at home is contingent on getting along with other members of the family and also with the neighbors. Even your health is directly affected by the way other persons affect you. So the project of awakening your own personal miracle power to help establish happy, harmonious relationships is essential to miracle-powered living.

Human beings are so interdependent that there is simply no way of being happy and successful without healthy human relationships. When you learn to work with miracle power, even long-standing conflicts and disturbances can be resolved, and new contacts can be started on the right basis. Miracle power does it through you!

What Do You See in Others?

As a start, you can learn something about yourself by noticing your reactions to other persons. Your attitude toward others is a sure indication of your feelings about yourself.

The more you genuinely like others, the more you like yourself. The more you appreciate their good qualities, the more you are developing these same qualities within yourself. It is always much easier to see in others those characteristics that are outstanding in yourself.

On the other hand, when you criticize and condemn others, you are really proving to the world that you are not very happy with your own life.

And if you see these things, you can take steps to do something about them.

Some people go through life searching out faults in others. They take a self-righteous pride in pointing to the wrongs that others have done. They consider themselves very superior persons because they haven't committed the sins they criticize. But they are forgetting one thing:

Thoughts are entities. They have power in themselves, and the thoughts which are directed primarily to error in the lives of others establish error in the mind of the thinker. Where there are strong thoughts of condemnation and criticism, there is no channel for miracle power to flow through.

"But," you say, "shouldn't I condemn wrong when I see it in others?"

Are you sure there is no wrong in your own life? Are you really in a position to judge? Have you never made a mistake, an error in thinking or acting? And, besides all that, can you afford to clutter your mind with critical, condemnatory thoughts that will cut off the miracle power?

There will be times that you will see wrong things done by others. In some cases you may be able to right a wrong at the time. But you can't afford to give yourself to contemplation of wrongs. When you do, you don't leave enough time or energy to establish the right. And that is your primary purpose here on earth, to establish good in your own life and in the lives that touch yours.

If your thoughts about other persons have made you unhappy or have led to disappointment and a critical attitude, now stop and reconsider. The thoughts you hold habitually about other persons indicate the thoughts you are holding about yourself. If you don't want to entertain that type of thinking about yourself, you must correct what you are thinking about others.

This is the principle of association.

You can always learn something about yourself by studying your reactions to others.

Neither Condemn nor Condone

You cannot emphasize errors in your mind by condemning them in others and still keep a clear channel for miracle power to flow through. Neither can you condone their wrong actions, agree with them in your mind, approve the mistake or error in ethics, and still be a good receiver for miracle power.

You are not to concentrate on the wrong at all. Rather, you will open the way for good by searching out good in others. Each person's potential always includes more good than you realize, and it is by looking past the wrongs and seeing his virtues that you awaken another's good qualities and good reaction to you. You don't really know what he is like as long as you concentrate on his bad side. Give him a chance to show a different nature, and you may be surprised to meet an entirely different personality in the same familiar face and form.

People do appear and act in different ways with different people. Their reaction has much to do with the way others think about them, or the way they think others think about them.

In one situation, a man may seem a hardheaded, domineering business man. At home, he may be a doting father or grandfather, and at social functions, he may display yet a third personality.

Of course, you will want to make sure that, as far as your personal contacts are concerned, you meet only the good side of his personality. You can do it. Miracles happen that even change other persons when you work with the miracle power in you.

You may have tried to make the changes first in other persons; it simply doesn't work. But you can learn to change others by first changing yourself. You don't have to start with their errors and correct them. You can begin with your thoughts and feelings about them, and correct those. There is a close interaction between your thoughts and the reactions of others. Change your thoughts, and you will change their reactions.

It may not happen immediately. Others have built a certain picture of you in their minds, and it may take time to change it. But if you are willing to work conscientiously to mentally and emotionally call forth the good qualities in others, you will find that you do get a response for your effort.

The principle of feeling works very strongly in relationships between individuals. It is this:

What you feel speaks louder than what you say.

Feelings Communicate Themselves

Love another person in spite of his faults, and, no matter how he resists it, something of your feeling gets through to him. If he feels guilty about some of the things he has done or is doing, he may even try to discourage your efforts to search out good in him, but he will feel your confidence and be blessed by it.

Hate another person, and even though you never say a word, something in him knows how you feel.

Sometimes people make a game of imagining conversations with persons they dislike, mentally making all the sarcastic remarks they would never dare say out loud. They may even form a mental caricature of the other person, so that they can laugh at him inside themselves, because they would never do it aloud. Maybe they imagine in detail incidents in which they get the best of the other person in a fight, or show him up in a contest of some type. They do this to compensate for feeling inferior in the other person's presence.

The details may not come through in contacts with those persons, but the thought and feeling do.

You can't afford to hold in your mind thoughts and feelings you would not communicate out loud, because thoughts and feelings do talk: they literally speak out loud, and other people hear them; sometimes the words and pictures you are holding in your mind make such a loud clamor that others can't hear a word you say; expressions of friendship are swallowed up in thought waves of hate.

Maybe on occasion you are silent when you would really like to tell another person what you think of him, but even silence is no protection. Sometimes it communicates much more than any words.

Since this is the case, you will do well to learn to hold in your mind those thoughts and feelings which will contribute to healthy personal relationships. You can, when you work with miracle power to help you establish right habits of thinking.

The Word Is "Good"!

Happy human relationships can be established by a word, and that word is "good"! It's much easier to get along with people when you are more aware of their virtues than their deficiencies.

Good is not a magic word, but it will make miracles happen in your life, because it makes miracles happen in your mind. Naming anything or any person good in your mind will mean that the situation can only bring good to you.

Even when others are hurt, you will be spared. Even when things go wrong in general, good will come to you. If you fill your mind with an awareness of good, other persons will be a part of the good in your life. It has to work that way. And no one can bring you less than good if you refuse to accept anything less in your mind.

Even when others seek to hurt you, they will not succeed if you continue to hold the good thought about them. Nothing can be less than good for you while you are holding the thought and the picture of good in your mind.

Even if you find it difficult to get along with another person, you can change your whole relationship by seeking out good in him. Call him good. Give him a genuine compliment occasionally. Think of him as good. Praise his good qualities. Associate him, in your mind, with good, and you will resolve difficulties first in your mind, and that is where it all begins.

If your mind is filled with thoughts of good, you will not be quick to take offense. Instead of asking resentfully, "What did he mean by that?" you will be recognizing, with understanding, "He probably had some reason for acting the way he did. He's really a good person."

And don't be afraid people will take advantage of you if you believe in their basic goodness! No one can take advantage of you unless you let it happen. When miracle power is flowing full force through your thoughts and feelings, it is so strong that it will protect you from any wrong that others might seek to do. It works like this:

A woman who lived alone answered her doorbell to discover a large, rough man standing there, threatening her with a knife as he sought to edge in the door.

Without fear and with pure goodness in her heart, she told him, "God loves you." She spoke it from the conviction deep within her. The man turned and ran. I never heard any more about him, but I feel sure that he was never quite the same after his contact with the little lady who knew she had nothing to fear from him. Such is the miracle power of faith in the good in other persons.

You Can't Afford Resentments

You can't afford not to believe good about others—for your own sake. Mentally, physically and emotionally, you need the protection and the understanding of believing in good.

Even resentments and grievances from the past must be cleared from your mind if you are to live richly, happily and successfully.

Remember the principle of association. You can't afford to hold thoughts about another that you don't want to see expressed in your life.

More than this, you can't afford to hold on to resentments because of what they do to you. They will affect your health. They will deplete your resources and decrease your ability to earn more. They will interfere with your ability to be happy. They will close the channels for your success.

You may think that you are hurting another person by refusing to forgive him. But you are hurting yourself most of all.

You can live harmoniously with other persons and with yourself, but only when you are big enough to forgive and forget the wrongs of the past, and those of the present as they occur.

As a matter of fact, you need bigness of outlook and attitude if you are to allow large supplies of miracle power to flow through and enrich your relationship with other persons.

You may have spoiled more than one friendship by taking offense at some small thing or by harboring resentment over an incident that really didn't matter, except as you thought about it and magnified it in your mind.

When you are on the lookout for slights and snubs and mental and emotional injuries of various types, you are sure to find them. You can always discover some cause for disturbance. But the disturbance is in you. Remember that. No one can perturb you unless you take the experience into yourself and become disturbed about it.

Things that might trouble you at one time will pass unnoticed at another, because of what is happening in you. If you are disturbed about one thing, or tired, or discouraged, some small incident can really get you down, because you are particularly susceptible at that time.

Of course, the answer lies in building such a strong, vital flow of miracle power that you are able to maintain your peace, your calm, your serenity, at all times and under all circumstances. You simply don't allow yourself to become upset, angry or resentful.

You understand, too, that you must maintain your balance, your poise, your inner peace, for your own sake. You cannot afford the results of inner conflict and disturbance. Nothing is important enough for you to upset yourself mentally, physically and emotionally.

Any emotional upheaval does affect you mentally, physically and emotionally. You find it more difficult to think clearly when you are disturbed. You experience actual physical reactions as the result of any emotional upset. You not only shut off the good that other persons could bring into your life, but you also close off the miracle power so tightly that you can't receive good from other persons or situations, either. You simply aren't able to let it through when you are concerned and upset.

Miracle power, of course, will help you to free yourself from these disturbing thoughts and the results of them.

"Miracle Power Is Greater"

You not only can be freed from the habit of accepting injury, but you also can be freed from the mental and emotional hurts of the past, and the results of your old mistakes in harboring resentments.

One method for being at home in your world, and at peace with yourself and your neighbor, is to know that you are greater than anything that happens to you. Learn to identify yourself with the same miracle power that regulates the universe, that keeps the stars in their places, that is behind every effect of law in your world, and you will find it easy to see the smallness of the things you have allowed to disturb you. And when you see how small they are, you can refuse to be troubled the next time.

If someone says something at which you might take offense, say to yourself, "Miracle power is greater than this. I am greater than this." Then switch your attention to something else and forget it. Or, better still, resolve what could have been a conflict with a compliment for the other person, or a pleasant remark of some kind. You may be surprised at how quickly and how easily bad tempers can be cured.

You don't have to work by yourself. That is why you can so easily accomplish the things that may have seemed impossible before.

You are no longer one little human being working alone against the world. You are a real person serving as an outlet for miracle power, which is tremendous and can do even the seemingly impossible thing through you.

Stop thinking as the little, puny human being and start knowing yourself as a powerhouse, and you won't have time for little, petty injuries in your relationship with others. You will have more important things to do than to argue or harbor resentments, or even take offense.

Free Yourself from Old Injuries

But what of those hurts that have come over from the past, those long-standing resentments that have colored your life and your outlook over a period of years?

Those may be a little more difficult to overcome, but they are not impossible. Nothing is impossible when you are working with miracle power.

Recognize this, and know that you must get rid of past resentments for your own peace of mind, and in order to get along happily with other persons. Then do it.

The principle of forgiveness is this:

Resentment binds you to wrong conditions and relationships. Forgiveness frees you from past wrongs and the conditions resulting from them.

For your own sake, you must forgive. And for the fulfillment of the over-all plan for your world, you must get rid of old, wrong feelings about other persons. You owe it to yourself, and you owe it to your Creator, who forgives you so many mistakes all the time.

No one needs to tell you what must be forgiven. No one knows, really, except you. But you are aware of those thoughts and feelings that are buried deep inside you, the hurt feelings, the resentments, the memories of injustice. You know what thoughts may haunt your thinking at times and make you keep asking, "Why? Why did he do it? Why did this happen to me?"

Take a look at these thoughts, these areas of disturbance, and then make up your mind to get rid of them, for your own sake if not for the sake of the person you feel has injured you. Decide definitely and finally that you don't want any old resentments cluttering up your thinking. And then relax away from them.

Concentrated thinking binds you to the wrongs that have been done and attracts other similar experiences to you. But you can't really think two thoughts at one time. So when you stop concentrating your thought power on the injury or injustice and start using it to emphasize beauty or good or great expectations for your life, the memory of the wrong becomes less and less important to you, until one day it simply isn't there any more.

One of the expressions of miracle power is through thought control. When you begin to work consciously with this power, you will learn that you can get rid of old, past hurts, even those things that you have thought you had to remember, you could never forget. You can, when you determine to do it, and let miracle power help you.

You can never have a completely happy personal relationship with anyone until you first have learned to seek out the good in everyone. And you will find tremendous changes taking place in you and in others as they relate to you when you free yourself from old resentments and the thoughts to which they have tied you.

You were created to contribute to your world, and you can contribute completely only when you are free of all false bonds, free to fulfill your divine destiny. Your thoughts and feelings about yourself and others determine where your life will lead you. When your thoughts and feelings are all directed toward love, harmony and peace, you will be contributing the most to yourself and to others. And, of course, you are always the one who benefits most.

Chapter 11

Stay Alive All Your Life

You are designed to live vitally all your life, not just to exist or get by, but to be vibrantly, radiantly alive, joyous, active and enthusiastic about life.

You were put here on earth not to deteriorate as the years pass, but to grow wiser, stronger and happier as time goes by. You should be happier and wiser now than you were ten years ago. Ten years from now, you should be happier and wiser still! Miracle power will help you do it.

Miracle power will make all the years of your life count for good —not just those few years that are designated as youth, but all the years of your life. The longer you live, the more experience you have had in living, and the more you should be able to give to life and to receive from life in return.

Youth Is a State of Mind

Youth is not a time of life; it is an experience of mind. You are as young or as old as you are thinking this moment, and you can become as youthful and vitally alive as you would like to be simply by changing your viewpoint. The principle of youth is this:

Youth is not a period of time, but a state of mind. You are as young, or as old, as you think.

The miracle of youth is yours for the claiming.

Not many people would choose to return to the problems and adjustments of the teens, but a youthful, happy attitude makes any years happy times of youthful activity and accomplishment.

You don't have to grow old! You can grow wiser as the years pass. You can grow more experienced in the business of living. You may mature in your attitudes toward yourself and other persons. But you don't have to age and lose interest in life and living.

Miracle power challenges you to stay alive all your life and to live more richly at eighty or ninety than you did at twenty or thirty. Miracle power is the true fountain of youth—not in some far-off place, but within you, waiting to be turned on and used by you as a part of successful, joyous living.

On his eightieth birthday Henry Kaiser, the industrialist, spoke of the new projects he was planning for the future. He had no ideas for retirement. Sanford Cluett, inventor of the preshrinking process called Sanforizing, put a new invention on the market when he was eighty.

What they did, you can do, or something more appropriate to your own particular interests and abilities. You can be just as young and vitally alive at eighty as you can think!

Aging is not the result of the number of years you have lived on this earth. It is the product of your thoughts, your attitudes, your feelings, and your acceptance or rejection of limitation.

In recent years scientists have discovered that man's body is self-renewing in such a way that there is no physical reason for aging. The cells, nerves, muscles and even the bones are constantly being replaced and renewed.

Diseases formerly blamed on age have come in for new study, and a committee appointed by the American Medical Association reported, "There are no diseases specifically resulting from the passage of a certain number of years." (AMA Committee on Aging Report, presented at AMA meeting, Los Angeles, Calif., November 1962)

Think Young!

You don't have to grow old! You will not age as long as you refuse to think old, to believe yourself old, or to look for the gray hairs and expect the spectacles that symbolize age. You are as young now as you can think, and you will continue to be just as youthful as you remain in your thoughts.

There are many ways in which you can cultivate a vital, youthful point of view.

Believe in good. Disillusionment and doubt are traits of aging. They manufacture wrinkles and take the sparkle from your eyes. But you don't have to allow such thoughts to make you look older. Believe in good, seek it out, and your faith in goodness will express itself as youth.

Courage is another quality that is necessary for a miracle-powered expression of youth. If you hold back for fear of failure, you will simply grow old without ever getting anywhere. If you are always entering into new experiences with joy and enthusiasm, the expression on your face will show how young you are in your thoughts. Not only that, but you'll leave those aging-failure thoughts behind and move into new and richer adventures in life.

Boredom leads to early aging. On the other hand, interest in life and living, interest in learning how to do new things, interest in participating in worth-while activities and aims, keeps you young at every age.

Say "Yes" to Life!

The one who is full of youthful vitality is the one who says "yes" to life. He may be eighteen, or he may be eighty. It is his joyous, enthusiastic participation in living that determines what he will receive from life, what he will give to it, and how he will live.

Miracle power flows fully and freely through you when you enter into life with joy and enthusiasm and a desire to live richly and productively all your time on earth.

Too many people refuse to say "yes" to life. They qualify their "yes" with all sorts of limitations.

They say, "It would be nice, but at my age——." Then they detail all the reasons for withdrawing from life after a certain number of years. They speak of a faulty memory, difficulty in moving about, or just a general giving up to the idea of old age.

Of course, if you say "yes, but," you are really saying "no" to the opportunities that are before you. You are using age as a sort of crutch, or excuse for withdrawing from life.

One with a youthful attitude says "yes" to new ideas, new experiences, new interests, new joy. And what he accepts, he has. Such is the activity of miracle power. All that you can claim for yourself at any age, you will experience.

You won't want to enter into and go forward with every project that is presented to you, but you must have a mind that is open to the possibilities and is willing to consider the propositions that come.

Instead of automatically meeting new ideas with a "yes, but" attitude, ask yourself these questions, and consider the answers honestly.

Is it right? Is it good? Is it capable of producing good? Will it hurt anyone? How do I feel about it, deep down inside? Do I believe I can succeed? Am I willing to do the work, to overcome the obstacles, to build a mental picture of success and fulfill it? Do I really want to do it?

You will be surprised at how much you can accomplish when you stop wasting energy on excuses and start doing the things that you would really like to accomplish. Miracle power will work with you when you start the activity with an expectant, interested attitude of mind.

The miracles that happen to people of seventy or eighty or ninety are not accidental. They are the result of an attitude of mind that is receptive to the activity of miracle power.

If you have found yourself limited in the past, stop saying "yes, but" and start answering "yes" to the opportunities life presents. Don't make excuses. Give each new project your interested consideration, choose those undertakings which are right and good for you, and enter into them with the enthusiasm that keeps you young at any age.

Interest Keeps You Young

Interest is essential to success, and interest is the key to maintaining a joyous, youthful approach to life. As long as you are interested, active, busy and enthusiastic, you are young in mind and body.

When you become bored, inactive, uninterested and lethargic, you naturally take on the aspects of age. But that doesn't have to happen. Miracle power, activated by your interest in new ideas, new concepts, new projects, will keep you young all your life!

Consider your topics of conversation. If you fall into the familiar pattern of talking about ailments, aging and other people's troubles, you are already set in the rut of age. But you can become interested in sparking your conversation with new, happy, bright items that interest you. If it interests you, most probably it will interest others as well, and if you talk with the bright, animated expression of enthusiasm, you become younger as you speak. It just works that way.

If you have fallen into one of those moods where it seems that nothing does stimulate you any more, even there miracle power can help you. When you desire to become interested, and search for something to awaken enthusiasm in you, miracle power will help you to do it.

Most people have had interests during their lives that they never had time to develop. If you find yourself bored or weary with life, go back and dust off some of those old hopes and desires. It is never too late to develop new areas of activity. And if the activities are ones that have been deferred for a long time, you have an even greater appreciation of the opportunity to develop new talents and abilities.

I have a friend who retired from a busy, productive life as a professional woman at the age of 75. Almost immediately, she signed up for a class in oil painting. She had always wished she could have time for this hobby and immediately went into it with enthusiasm.

Then she decided it would be nice to do some sort of volunteer work, so that she could feel a sense of contributing to the good of others. She started working as a Red Cross counselor one or two days a week.

She is now in her eighties and is one of the busiest, happiest people I know. Interest is the key—interest in others, interest in new ideas, new things, new projects. Interest and enthusiasm awaken greater and greater quantities of miracle power, and they widen the channel through which it flows, until it blesses not just one life, but many.

Changing Interests Bring New Experiences

Your interests may change as you live a certain number of years, but a curiosity about new areas of life and living and a desire to participate will continue to give you a successful, happy experience in living.

The sports that intrigued you in earlier years may take a back seat after you live a certain length of time, but they should be replaced by other interesting, stimulating diversions.

The work you do may change as you change and grow through experience. Your recreation and hobbies may be different. But through the change, there should be a current of interest, so that the activities in your life continue to be adventures in living.

If at some time you find yourself falling into a rut and losing the joy of living, do some active work on arousing enthusiasm, searching out new projects or activities that do stimulate you mentally and physically. If you truly desire to be interested and to live fully and happily all your life, you will be shown the way in which you can keep yourself vitally alive and miracle-powered for rich living at any age.

As you grow happier and wiser, rather than older, you will find that each day brings its own challenges, but it also carries its own joy and satisfaction in successful accomplishment. Where there is interest, each day holds new ideas, new beauty, new awareness of love and friendship, and new experiences of good.

Life is to be lived not just at certain times or for certain periods, but all of the time all your life.

It doesn't matter how old you are as you read this. You are as old, or as young, as you are thinking right now. And you can be as young all the rest of your life as you will start thinking now. Make interest a vital part of your youthful thought.

Start where you are (you can't start anywhere else, anyway), and think young, be young, live and enjoy it!

Learn the Art of Enjoyment

Living richly all your life is not a matter of preparing for your old age from the time you leave the teen years. It is, rather, a matter of growing into the new experiences that are the special blessings of each part of life, each era of activity through which you pass—growing through them and then releasing them as you go into the next phase of life.

Many times young people show more interest in the pension plan and old-age benefits than in the job they are considering. They are more concerned with the idea of security in their old age than they are with the interest offered by the work they will be doing for the next forty years. If you aren't interested in the earlier years, how can you expect to suddenly start enjoying life when you retire?

Interest in life and enthusiasm for living are qualities that you build through use and practice. The more you enjoy your work during your most active years, the more interests you will find to make the years of retirement happy and productive.

Sometimes young parents look forward to the day when their children will be married and settled in homes of their own. They feel that then they will have time to enjoy themselves.

There is a particular opportunity in every time of life. If you want to enjoy the later years of freedom, take time to learn the art of enjoyment when the children are small. Enjoy their growth along with your own, and you will be ready for each phase of new activity as it comes.

Every time of life brings its own special gifts, its challenges and opportunities. Every day of your life is to be lived, not simply endured. You can't skip it. So why not enjoy it?

Keep your interest high in life where you are. Don't wait until some future time. Learn how to be interested, active and enthusiastic about whatever you are doing, and then carry this talent with you as you go, becoming richer all the time as you become more adept in the art of living.

Miracle-powered living is based on interest.

Life's Bonuses

Another key to enjoyment of your later years (and all your life, for that matter) lies in participation in life's extras, those little bonuses that life is constantly offering you.

Here, again, it is well to learn how to accept these dividends as you go along. Then you will be skilled in the art of accepting them later, and you will have had the privilege of enjoying them all along.

Many people miss the joy of living during the years that they are busy making a living. And, when they retire, they find they haven't learned how to collect these dividends of enjoyment.

A popular song of several years ago said, "The best things in life are free!"

Miracle power will help you discover those little extra qualities of life that have no price tag. These things can be had for the asking, or the claiming, but all too few people remember to stop and ask.

There is nothing wrong with working; this is a part of man's fulfillment. There is nothing wrong with attaining a certain position in life, or making money; success and prosperity are a part of man's heritage. But these phases of life should be established in their right relationship to other goals of living.

Take time to enjoy the beauty of a rose blooming, or even of a daffodil. Don't hurry through life so fast that you fail to see the loving smile that is given, or the tentative offer of friendship. Let life's extras, those things that are free, be a part of your daily experience. The more you welcome them into your life, the richer you will be. Work is not all of living, and neither is position.

Are you finding time for enjoyment of simple things? For sharing? For growing? For learning? If not, then let miracle power help you to discover a new and wonderful experience in living as you search out "the best things in life"—the ones that are free.

As a very wise Man said many years ago, life is more than clothing and food. It is also more than shelter and social position. Put these parts of life in their proper place, but don't let them monopolize all of your attention. Take time to accept life's extras, too. They will enrich the present, and the future as well.

Grow Happier and Wiser

Work with joy and interest, take time to enjoy life's dividends, and refuse to become burdened by the years as they pass. If you are working with miracle power, the years will pass so quickly and so happily that you won't really have time to accumulate them as a burden.

Burdens are not a part of God's plan for your life. They are something you make, or accept, for yourself. Make up your mind to be free, and you are free! Even the passing of years should not be a burden.

Look at it this way: Most of the burdens man carries through life are not physical, but mental. They are a hindrance he creates for himself, in his mind. And as they are manufactured in the mind, they can be released there as well.

It isn't a physical problem, a circumstance, an obligation or the passing of a certain number of years which burdens you. It is your attitude toward it, and your thought about it.

A man who was crippled by infantile paralysis became President of the United States. A musician who had lost his hearing continued to write compositions that are considered classics. Others have ignored what many people consider the burden of old age to accomplish greater work in their later years than they did when they were young.

There is no burden until, or unless, you accept it.

Your body should not become a burden as you grow older. Your mind should stay alert and active. Don't accept the idea of the burden of a poor memory because you have lived a certain number of years on earth.

You are a powerhouse. You are a potential powerhouse at any time at any age. You have within you a direct line to release all the miracle power you can accept and use, all you can conduct through your mind and your body.

This has nothing to do with your age. The longer you live, the more accomplished you should become in the use of this power to make miracles the order of the day in your life.

Remember: you are as young, or as old, as you think. If you aren't thinking young at the present time, then use the miracle methods to change your thought.

Get rid of the belief in burdens of any kind. Become interested, enthusiastic, joyous and stimulated by the wonders of life, the extras, the fulfillment of work, the challenges of each day.

Give your full attention to living richly and fully where you are now, with a full free flow of miracle power activating your mind and body. Don't grow older and weaker. Just grow happier and wiser.

Miracle power will help you to do it.

Chapter 12

Use It and Watch It Grow

You are created to be the master of yourself and of conditions in your world. You are designed for health, prosperity and success. You are made to produce good in quantities not yet imagined by man, and you are to be happy and free while doing it.

All the equipment you can ever need or use has already been given to you. And with it has come the privilege of choice.

You can choose just how much of the miracle power you will use in your life. No one will force it on you, and no one can keep it away. It is there for you, whether or not you ever claim it. Miracles can happen to you anywhere at any time that you plug in to the miracle power. And they will happen when you do. No one can stop them.

There is another interesting point about miracle power. You can never use it up. Just the reverse is true. The more you use, the more you have, because it is by use that you open the channels wide so that the power can pour freely into your life through the way you have opened for it.

Learn the principles on which miracles are based. Study them. Understand them. And even if you don't understand them completely, start applying them in your life. The more you use the knowledge you have, the more you work with the principles you can understand even a little, the more you will have of miracle power working in and through you.

Understanding Brings Responsibility

With your understanding of the working of miracle power comes responsibility. The more you know, the more you are responsible for using.

Don't start to change your life through the activity of miracle power unless you are serious about making it work for you. You can't expect to use just a little when you happen to need it, and forget it the rest of the time. Miracle living is a full-time project, but it is the most fulfilling, satisfying project you will ever undertake.

One of the miracle laws is this, the principle of use:

If you fail to use anything, be it talent, tool or knowledge, you will lose even that which you have. But, if you use what you have now for good, it will grow!

You will be surprised at how rapidly the miracle power in your life can grow when you start where you are to use what you know now. Go back and review some of the principles you have learned in this book and then put them to work. Even if you don't see just how they can work, even if you aren't quite sure they will work, even though you can't understand them completely, begin to use them at your present level of understanding. And watch your understanding grow with the miracle power!

The more you co-operate with universal law and release the universal power in your life, the more you will broaden your world, and the more you will participate in the over-all plan of good for all men everywhere.

You are a powerhouse! And a powerhouse is to be used to fulfill its right and proper purpose. Your purpose is to live richly and happily and to produce good to enrich the lives of others as well as your own life.

You are needed to help fulfill the universal plan. It is not an accident that you are where you are at this particular time. You are where you are because there are things there to be done. You are given all the miracle power you need to do those things.

When you begin to work with these ideas, you may even think of yourself as small and insignificant in God's over-all plan for the universe. But as your interest grows, as you learn to apply the miracle principles, you will see new and exciting areas of discovery unfolding for you. You will find new methods of service, and you will enlarge your present contribution to your world. You will begin to fit yourself, mentally and spiritually, into a larger concept and a greater project in living. You will bless others. But you will be blessed most of all. This is the way miracle power works.

The Way It Works

Use it, or lose it.

In a few words, this is the law. You must use the knowledge you have, the talents you have developed, the muscles you have been employing, or you will lose even that which you have had.

You have undoubtedly been through the experience of failing to use a certain talent for a while, and discovering that you had lost much of your proficiency. If you don't practice the piano, swim or solve difficult equations, you will find that your ability to do so has diminished. So you make it a point to keep in condition or practice in those areas where you must continue to perform with efficiency.

Make the use of your miracle power, your universal energy, one of the top-priority projects in your life. Once you have awakened this power in your life, you can't afford to live without it. Not only that, but you will find a deep-down urge to continue to expand your life into new and wonderful areas of expression. Something in you will keep you dissatisfied unless you do exercise your spiritual muscles regularly, unless you activate the universal laws in your life in such a way that miracles become the order of every day.

You will not be satisfied to see an occasional miracle; you will want to put these higher laws into operation all the time, because you know how miracle power works!

Don't wait for some tremendous need to use the miracle power. Turn it on any time, all the time, for small needs as for large ones, or even just because you feel the need to grow in mind and to participate in life.

Develop your understanding of miracle power by quiet times of meditation and examination of just what it is, what it is all about, how it works and how you can work with it. But don't be content with thinking about it; use it. Make it a part of all of your life all the time. The more you use, the more you will have.

You have been given all the miracle-power potential you can ever use, and more. Your part is to continue to open the way for it to work, and you do this by consciously co-operating with the universal laws on your highest level of understanding at the present time, and then increasing that understanding.

Use it, and you'll never lose it. It will grow stronger, and you will grow richer, day by day. You are a powerhouse, and it is your job to turn on the power!

"Where's the Fruit?"

Don't become impatient if you are not able to achieve those things you would like to do the first time you try. Unlimited miracle power is yours to claim, but you must learn to use it first in order to open the channels through which it comes.

Definite faith and action on your part will change your life immediately, but perhaps you will not attain all your goals as quickly as you would like.

One of the miracle laws is the law of growth. The principle of growth is this:

All great things grow, by a natural and orderly process, from small beginnings.

Most people are willing to accept the idea that growth in nature is gradual and orderly. They are perfectly content to wait for the baby to become a boy, and the boy to become a man. They plant the seed of a flower or a vegetable, and wait patiently for it to break through the earth, increase in size, and then produce fruit according to its nature.

However, the same people who wait patiently for growth to take place in nature's own outer ways are not so understanding when it comes to changing their lives by changing their minds. They plant the seed of a new idea and then ask, "Where's the fruit?"

Ideas must grow, too. They are planted as seeds in your mind.

Then they must be nurtured as they go through the process of growth. Sometimes they require transplanting as your understanding gives you new insight. They grow to maturity and produce fruit in your life, but they must be cultivated while they are in the process of becoming that which they are to be.

It is not enough just to give a little time and attention occasionally to those things you would like to realize in your life. Anything worth achieving is worth the time and attention that are required for its right growth and development, first as an idea in mind and later as an expression of that basic concept.

Many people, learning the laws of mind for the first time, feel that they can start with the full-grown expression of the good they desire. They think the whole process sounds pretty easy. They will apply a few simple rules, and the result will take care of itself.

But all life is growth, and this is true in the study of miracle power as in anything else.

You have to learn, and to grow with the knowledge, in order to make miracle principles work for you. They are true, and they are dependable, but they must be applied in the orderly way that is the base of all nature, the process of growth.

You can be sure that the moment you activate miracle power in your life by changing your mind and opening the way for it to express itself, you are a different person. You will see some changes soon, if you don't see them immediately.

But don't spoil all your progress with impatience. Be willing to learn, to grow, to open the channels for miracle power to come through, and to let the order of the universe be established in your life.

All great things grow, by a natural and orderly process, from small beginnings.

You are designed to bring forth the great things, and you are equipped by miracle power to do all that you need to do. Co-operate with the laws of the universe according to your own best understanding at the present time, and you will grow into those greater experiences of health, joy and accomplishment, or whatever you are seeking to achieve by miracle methods.

Use it, and watch it grow!

Practice Is a Key

Someone has said, "Knowledge is a treasure, but practice is the key to it."

Practice is a key to the use of miracle power, not because it is required by the Source of the power, but because you must learn how to use it in order to draw on the supply.

What would happen if an electric-power plant were turned over to a child to operate? The results could be disastrous!

With miracle power goes the responsibility for using it rightly, and it is turned on in greater quantities as you prove your ability and responsibility through practice.

Don't be afraid to use the knowledge you have. Don't be afraid to step out on faith and see if it will work. Even when your faith is not yet full-grown, you can make miracles happen by working with the principles of the universe. This is the only way that you will ever build the great faith and the great ability to work intelligently with the laws.

All it takes is a little knowledge to begin the practice of miracle living. But if you can quote this book from cover to cover, but have never tried to use the knowledge it contains, you haven't really benefited.

Miracle living is yours for the claiming, and one way in which you claim miracle power is through practice at your present level of understanding.

Go back to one of the early principles. You may not understand all of the principle of recognition, but you can work on it, right where you are. See that you can draw on a power greater than anything you have ever yet experienced. Convince yourself that the power is there, and that it is possible for you to bring it forth. Then do it. Choose another principle, and go to work on that.

Miracle power is yours for the releasing, but practice opens the channels through which it flows.

The more familiar you become with the laws of living, and the more you see miracles happen as you consciously activate the power, the stronger you become as a working dispenser of power.

Knowledge is nothing until it is used. Practice what you know, and watch it grow.

Start with a Small Job

You don't have to wait for great opportunities in order to test what you know. You can use even a universal principle for small things as well. These laws are true, and they apply in little cases as well as large ones.

It is through using the power, even while doing everyday tasks, that you perfect your technique and prepare the way for greater success and achievement.

Recall the principle of vision. Know that whatever you can see yourself doing, you can do. You might want to try this first on a small repair job, something that you have put aside because it seemed difficult but not impossible.

Visualize yourself doing the work. Go through every step in your mind. Open yourself to new concepts and new approaches. And, when you can see the job completed in your mind, then start it. You will wonder why you waited so long.

Friedrich von Schiller said one time, "Only those who have the patience to do simple things perfectly, will acquire the skill to do difficult things easily."

This is true in writing plays. It is true in developing a musical talent, or in building skill in cleaning or repairing or any other specialty. It is also true in miracle living. The more you use your knowledge in small things, the more you will have available for those large opportunities that arise.

Don't ask your friends what you should do, and don't waste time and energy in explaining your plans to them. Just get busy right where you are and use miracle power and miracle principles for everything that comes up in your day. You'll be surprised at how easily difficulties will smooth themselves out, and how quickly your understanding and ability grow. That, too, is the working of law, the laws of use and growth.

And don't forget—the miracle power you use in small ways increases to fill your big needs.

"You Have to Start Now!"

After the last game of the season, a reporter asked Deacon Jones of the Los Angeles Rams what he thought his team would do the next season.

The football player declined to predict whether the Rams would win the championship another year, but he did comment, "You can't start preparing for next year next year; you have to start now!"

Those things which you want to do in the future, even those things you predict as you begin to employ miracle power, are always dependent on what you are doing today.

The time to put miracle power to work in your life is not next year, or even next week. It is now, today, where you are. There will never be a better time.

Make plans for the future. Let your vision take you into new and wonderful areas of expression. But lay the groundwork for it today. Football practice doesn't start the day before the big game. The crowd that cheers the team on, or boos it, may not even think of the hours that have gone into preparation for the event, but it is practice, preparation and attitude that determine the outcome of the football game, or the game of living.

You can put yourself in training for miracle living right now. And you can reap rewards of success along the way, as you prepare for those bigger opportunities to come.

Remember Your Spiritual Powerhouse

You are a physical powerhouse.

You are a mental powerhouse.

You are a powerhouse of talent and ability.

Start where you are, and you can release volumes of miracle power to make you healthy, strong, active, wise, prosperous, successful and filled with the joy of living.

But if you want to experience the greatest benefit of the miracle methods, remember that you are also a spiritual powerhouse. You are a spiritual powerhouse, and you have a direct line to the Source.

The universal principles work. They will work for you, whether or not you ever credit the Source of all good. But if you want the greatest results in your life, learn to turn on the spiritual power. Practice prayer. Get to know the One who made you in His image and likeness. Take time to feel His presence and His power. Listen to His ideas. Ask His advice and guidance as you seek a greater understanding and working knowledge of His laws.

Don't limit yourself to just a mental and physical acceptance of the power, but go all the way. Turn it on spiritually as well.

Don't be stingy about letting God into your life, reserving your acquaintance for certain times and places.

Turn on the spiritual power and let it flow. Let it build. Let it expand. Let it work through you not only to establish those miracles which you can visualize now, with your present understanding, but also to open the way for greater service, greater blessings, greater good for yourself and everyone you contact.

The more you recognize God at work in all of His universe, the easier you will find it to actively work with the power from which miracles are made.

As you make your own miracles by understanding and co-operating with the laws of the universe, you will recognize that they are not really your own at all. They are God's miracles which you have simply learned to accept and receive into your life.

You are here not just to make miracles happen for your own benefit; you are here to open the way for more good to come into the world for others as well.

Miracle power cannot be confined by selfish interests, but it will flow freely when it is used to implement God's plan of good for all persons.

Learn the miracle principles. Turn on the miracle power. Make miracles an everyday occurrence in your life. But don't stop there. Let yourself be used by a higher power to bring miracles to others as well. When you do, you will find that the miracle power pours through you in such quantities that it literally carries you along into new and greater experiences of good.

You can never give it away. And, when you use it under divine direction, you will be surprised at the way it can grow!